CAPT. CAMPBELL'S
"POEM IN STEEL."

New Wonder Car Capable of Doing 220 M.P.H.

SMALL ENGINE NEEDED TO START IT.

CAPTAIN Malcolm Campbell, who holds the British motor speed record, is going to America shortly to attack the world's speed record of 203 miles an hour established by Major Segrave.

A £20,000 motor-car, described as "a poem in steel," has been built for this purpose, and it is claimed that it can attain a speed of 220 m.p.h.

The secret engine is s
won the Schneider Trophy,
power can be gained from
ngine is required to start i
Campbell will make

12-CYLINDER
ENGINE.

Great Power
ebird

TO S
CORD

By the Gazette's Motoring Correspor
Secrets of Captain Malcolm Camp
monster car of many wonders, which
of the greatest engineering experts
country have helped to construct.
revealed yesterday at the works of M
Napier and Sons, at Acton, Lo
Bluebird, as the car is called, will
for America on the Berengaria
February, to take part in the great
national carnival for the world's
records at Daytona Beach, where Ca
Campbell will defend for Britain, a
American challengers, Major Seg

CAPT. CAMPBELL'S 220 M.P.
CAR FOR DAYTONA RACE.

New Blue Bird To Attack World Sp
Record Held By Major Segrave.

900-H.P. AERO ENGINE.

Monster As Easy To Con
As A Light Car.

es a minute on land! Something approaching
will be attained in the International Car Race at
, Florida, next month, if Capt. Malcolm Camp
Bird, which has cost him £20,000 to build, justifi

d the veil of secrecy which has enshro
mechanical projectile,

with an engine similar to that in Web
der Cup plane; and, with its long, lean
fin," resembles some steel monster fr
ance.

m speed is being kept secret, but is bel
hbourhood of 220 miles an hour—well
world record of 203 m.p.h.

WORLD SPEED KING ON HIS TRIUMPH.

"THOUGHT I WAS GONE."

ROADSIDE SKID AT
MILES AN

S MOTORING SPEED RECORD
AGAIN BROKEN.

MPBELL'S GREAT ACHIEVEMENT IN FLORIDA.

DRIVER'S BRAVERY AND TO BRITISH CAR
CONSTRUCTION.

Florida) message states that Capt. Malcolm Campbell set up a new world record
in his Napier "
established by Maj
ion.
February 4, 1927—
174.224 miles per

ne was 170.624 mil
ird," cost £18,000
wins the 1,000-gu
he end of 1930, giv
e news," said Sir C
Englishman. It is
I saw his machine.

be in a position to meet the American
Captain Campbell to

FASTEST MOTO
HOME AGAIN

CAPT. CAMPBELL REL
HIS EXPERIENCE

MAJOR SEGRAVE
AND
CAPT. CAMPBELL.

HIGH SPEED LURE.

JOINT ATTEMPT AT
NEW RECORD?

By THE MOTORING

CAPTAIN CAMPBELL
HOME AGAIN.

PLANS TO MAKE 'BLUE BIRD'
FASTER STILL.

FROM OUR SPECIAL CORRESPONDENT.
SOUTHAMPTON, Friday.
"I may have another try to go
faster still. I have learnt a lot.
The Blue Bird will do more when
I make some modifications which I have

HINT OF ATTEMPT
BEAT HIS RECO

Kaleidoscope series

LIFE WITH THE SPEED KING

By Leo Villa

With assistance from Kevin Desmond

Foreword by
Mrs Jean Wales (née Campbell)

PUBLISHED BY
MARSHALL HARRIS & BALDWIN LTD
17 AIR STREET LONDON W1

THE AUTHORS

ALTHOUGH Leo Villa has recounted vividly the events of his life from 1899 to 1935 in this book, the second half was to be just as active. From 1936 to 1948, he acted as chief engineer and racing mechanic to Sir Malcolm Campbell for the *Bluebird* single-step hydroplane and the *Bluebird* three-pointer, working beside Loch Lomond, Lago Maggiore, Lake Hallwyl and Coniston Water - the backbone to Sir Malcolm's four world water speed records (126.33 mph, 129.5 mph, 130.93 mph and 141.74 mph). On On Malcolm's death, Leo switched his unfailing loyalty and unequalled engineering experience to Donald and at the time of the latter's tragic death on Coniston Water in January 1967 had acted as chief engineer for a further seven water speed records (202-276 mph) and a land speed record (403 mph). Aged 67, he had served the Campbells for 45 years and 22 world speed records.

During the last twelve years of his life, he was able to spend a great deal more time with his wife Joan - and his recreations were lecturing, high-speed motoring in his red Triumph GT6 sports car, gardening and writing, surrounded by many unique mementoes of his former achievements. His first, sparsely illustrated autobiography *The Record Breakers*, written with Tony Gray, was published by Paul Hamlyn in 1969 and sold out in both English and French language editions.

It was at this point that he met with Kevin Desmond, who was to assist him in the writing that he was to complete during the next decade of his life. Kevin has recalled:

'Our first joint effort was *The World Water Speed Record*, published by B T Batsford in 1976. This was followed by a chain of boating articles and also the *Leo Villa Remembers* series in the original *OLD MOTOR*. Our system was that Leo would burn the midnight oil, writing out his recollections in long-hand capital letter words (usually in biro), then I would take his manuscript and, in his own words, "do all the bits and pieces" - word order, grammar, spelling, punctuation, etc. When he started writing, Leo's style was somewhat stilted and awkward, but I can honestly say the literary craftsmanship as appears in *LIFE WITH A SPEED KING* left me with hardly any room for improvement. Considering the conditions under which he wrote the manuscript, this achievement is all the more remarkable'.

PREFACE

ON the surface, Leo Villa's life of speed and excitement might read like something from the pages of *Boys' Own Paper* if he had not been such a charming and modest man. As it is, the text he wrote to accompany this unique photographic record of his working life with the happy-go-lucky Giulio Foresti and the perfectionist Malcolm Campbell is one of the most remarkable records of its type. We share in the excitements and disappointments of the vintage days of motor racing and go behind the scenes in Campbell's ceaseless quest for speed - not speed for its own sake or for personal glory, but for the prestige it could bring to his beloved Britain.

Leo Villa was content to slip into the shadows in his descriptions of those exciting days, and apart from the odd grumble about frequent burning of the midnight oil, or being set some impossible tasks in impossible locations, he is happy to let the cars and their owners take the glory. From the achievements of the Campbells we can tell what an accomplished mechanic Leo Villa must have been, and reading between the lines in his amusing and perceptive photograph captions we can gauge a little of the immense contribution he made to the design and tuning of the Campbell cars. On the face of it, Leo Villa had one of the most exciting jobs in the history of fast motoring and he plainly enjoyed it to the full. At the same time we realise the total devotion that he gave to his work and the bond that grew between him and his remarkable employer, whose life so often depended on the workmanship, skill and forethought of his trusted servant.

It was a most unusual relationship, yet one which endured for two generations of Campbells, and some superhuman feats of speed and endurance. The likes of the Campbells and Leo Villa are unlikely to be seen again, and we can only be thankful that this unique pictorial record and personal memory remains.

FOREWORD

AS the daughter of Sir Malcolm Campbell, I knew Leo Villa for some 56 years, which is only two years less than my brother, the late Donald Campbell. As a little girl, I well remember how Leo built toys for us, such as a wonderful rabbit hutch with the words *Maison Bunnee* written overhead, and repaired our bicycles and Donald's steam-engined train.

In later years, when I was old enough to appreciate what my father and then my brother were achieving on both land and water, I soon discovered how very much Leo's hard work of preparation had helped towards their successes. And when, sadly, both men had made their final record attempts, Leo was left, like myself, with so many nostalgic flash-backs to the *Bluebird* era.

Today there has grown up a small library of about a dozen books which have been written about my near family - three of them *by* my family - and now this *KALEIDOSCOPE*, which was Leo's third authorship, not to mention the many magazine articles he wrote and the lectures he gave to keep the Campbell name alive. When we knew him, the Campbells would never have dreamt that Villa might become an author!

They say that one good picture is worth a thousand words, and what makes this book so very special are its carefully selected 170 photos, many of which have, for me, vividly brought back many a happy and exciting memory of pre-war days spent at Brooklands and elsewhere.

As a Chevalier of the Order of St John of Malta, a Freeman of the City of London, and with an OBE after his name Leo had become a legend in his own lifetime, an inspiration for any on-going or future Land or Water Speed Records. He had even been given a special mention in *The Guinness Book of Records* as 'Champion Mechanic'. To me, however, he will always remain as he appears in this book, just plain Leo Villa, a very close friend of the Campbell family.

If you turn to the back of this book you may read of how Leo died - at almost the same time of day as he had been born, and the same time of day as he had spent working on those infernal engines. It has been a great sadness - me in particular - that Leo didn't live to see the publication of this book. My only consolation is that at least he is still living in its pages.

MRS JEAN WALES *née* Campbell
[*Photograph taken in May 1947 shows Miss Jean Campbell, Sir Malcolm Campbell and Lord Howe.*]

A COCKNEY CHILDHOOD

From a cosmopolitan background and an early career in London's Italian
restaurant community, Leo Villa joined Foresti's Itala agency before the Great War.
Following service as an Air Mechanic with the Royal Flying Corps,
where he became familiar with many of the types of engine
to be seen in later Brooklands and Record cars, Leo rejoined Foresti
and headed for the exciting world of Continental motor racing.

0   My father, Leopoldo Mauritzio Villa, was born in Lugano, Switzerland - also his brother Ferdinando. By contrast, my mother, *née* Adelaide Florence Hawkins, was born at Greenock in Scotland. My Swiss grandfather was the captain of the paddle steamer *Ceresio* [Cherry], which transported its many passengers to and from the many - then small - villages dotted around the Lugano lakeside.

I, Leopoldo Alfonso Villa, was brought into the world some two hours after midnight on 30th November 1899. Not only born at that unearthly hour, I also appear to have spent many a 'wee small hour' since then repairing blown-up racing car engines or seeking those elusive bonus rpms!

My mechanical aspirations, no doubt, originated from my grandfather, Capitano Villa, and subsequently flamed into action through Uncle Ferdie, who was one of the pioneer everyday motorists.

The family group shown here is of my father, mother and sister Amalia [Millie]. I also had a younger brother, Ferdie, who arrived later. I think this 'Cabinet Portrait' was taken in 1901-02 when I was two years old.

1   Some of my earliest memories are of my Uncle Ferdie's early acquisition which was, I believe, a Globe motor bicycle, manufactured about 1902. It was a brute to start and on many occasions - with Uncle pedalling like the devil - accompanied by some of my boyhood friends, we would push him round and round Soho Square. After a series of pops and bangs, the engine started up and off he went, leaving us all standing breathless. Once underway, Uncle would keep careering round the Square for fear of the engine stopping and his being abandoned without our continued support!

2   The Palace Theatre, Cambridge Circus, within a stone's throw of my birthplace. I still recollect the large posters advertising 'Anna Pavlova - The Greatest Ballerina of All Time', who was appearing there. To the left is Shaftesbury Avenue, and further down on the left, not shown, is the old Shaftesbury Theatre, then showing a play called *The Arcadians*. Both these theatres were situated on their own sites so that, at times, long queues encircled three sides of each theatre. Apart from the old barrel-organ, these eager theatre-goers would be kept entertained by street performers, buskers, acrobats, conjurers, etc.

Roller-skating had come into vogue by the time I had reached the age of eight. It became a rage with the street boys in the Soho district and after a great deal of persuasion, my father condescended to buy me a pair of skates. Although they afforded me much pleasure, I was not particularly proud of them - as opposed to the more elite types, owned by some of my friends, these were called 'ankle-breakers', and were purchased for 1/11½d from Marks & Spencer, then trading in Berwick Street near Berwick Market. The more expensive type of skates owned by my friends were fitted with wheels running on ball-bearings, the axles being attached to a rubber mounting which, like a universal joint, allowed the direction of the wheels to follow the thrust line of the foot. When in motion, my so-called 'ankle-breakers' lacked these fineries, most certainly reducing and limiting my performance.

3 Also on the left-hand side of Shaftesbury Avenue, opposite the Palace Theatre, was the London Salvage Corps station. This photograph is not of the station in question, but is remarkably similar to the one situated near my birthplace.

In the aftermath of a fire or accident, the station doors would be flung open and the horse-drawn engines would race out. The din from the clatter of the horses' hooves, the iron-clad wheels on the hard roadways, coupled with the clanging of the hand-manipulated warning bells was something I shall never forget.

4 Piccadilly 1910, with horse traffic a-plenty and one solitary taxi bringing up the rear. The Law moves in, with the street ambulance used in those days to convey possibly the unfortunate victim of a street accident to the nearest hospital. On the other hand, it could have been one of the more violent baddies or drunks who roamed the streets at the time, being taken to Marlborough Street Police Station.

5 My family had moved from London to Kennington at the outbreak of the 1914-1918 War. I was 15 at the time and had left my old school, St Martin-in-the-Fields. I had spent several weeks doing practically nothing with several of my new friends, when my father decided it was time I put my hands to good account; he found me a situation as pageboy at Romano's Restaurant in the Strand. My father had been working for Alfonso Nicolino Romano for a number of years and had formed a great attachment for his boss. Possibly my middle Christian name being Alfonso had a bearing on this. Incidentally, my father was a *sommelier* of unusual talent and very popular with the clientele he served. Mr Romano - or 'The Roman' as he was known - died during 1901. Later I was engaged by the manager at that time, Luigi Naintree. I disliked the job intensely and was relieved of my post some months later when, during a contretemps with the hall porter, I grabbed the hall inkpot and tipped it over his well-groomed cranium.

6 Almost opposite Romano's stood the old Tivoli Theatre, a popular music hall where many well-known actors of the time appeared. In the right-hand corner can be seen one of the very early cinemas - 'The Cinema de Luxe'. For some reason or other, we would call it the Bioscope. This was the first cinema I had ever visited and when we were living in London our weekly treat was to be taken to the Bioscope. I vividly remember the square metal tickets doled out by the cashier on entry, the musical tones of the piano, and the varying tempo of music played to suit the picture being shown - especially if it were a *belle* heroine being tied down to a railway line before an oncoming express train!

7 Showing the top end of the Strand, approaching Fleet Street and the Law Courts of Justice, then the old Gaiety Theatre with Kingsway on its left side. The road on the bottom right-hand corner leads you to Waterloo Bridge. This picture was taken about 1910 and sums up the tranquillity and carefree mode of those days. As can be seen, the old twin cylinder Renault taxi was a popular form of transport for the more wealthy businessman, as opposed to the cheaper mode of travel by horse-drawn bus, or the motor buses that were now beginning to make their appearance for public transport. Horse-drawn cabbies would often sarcastically refer to motor cabbies as 'bloody gardeners'! We would refer to the Renault taxis as 'two-funnelled jobs'!

8   My premature termination of employ as a pageboy at Romano's caused my father some concern, and had it not been for the timely intervention of my Uncle Ferdie, who was then manager of Pagani's Restaurant in Great Portland Street, my introduction into the now expanding mechanical world might never have come about. Giulio Foresti, the well-known Itala car specialist and racing driver, was a great friend of my Uncle and it was arranged that I should go and work for Signor Foresti. I was given the opportunity of often working on a job with the Maestro himself; he was a brilliant engineer and I was soon to learn quite a lot about the Itala models that were his stock-in-trade, in particular the 50 and 90hp rotary valve types. Regrettably, the tempo of the European conflict had increased considerably and all too soon I had to leave Foresti to enroll for military service. I was seventeen at the time.

9 With some trepidation I was hustled into a room at a recruiting office in Lambeth where, without ceremony, I was conducted to a desk behind which sat a burly-looking type, wearing the King's uniform. In a gruff but anything but pleasant tone, he asked me several questions, his focal point being my name and its foreign origin. My sense of self assurance completely deserted me when, in no uncertain terms, I was told to address him as 'Sir'. However, after being duly passed medically fit, being sworn in and receiving the King's shilling, in due course I had to report at an Army depot near Hampton Court. My first night was spent in a hut with some other raw recruits like myself. I can still vaguely remember the foul atmosphere caused by a smelly coke-fired stove and tobacco smoke, and the commanding voice of a sergeant major who appeared to be making a small fortune out of a number of the chaps with his wretched Crown & Anchor board.

We were subsequently despatched to Talavera Barracks at Aldershot and within weeks I was posted to Halton Camp, Wendover, Bucks, to be put through a trade test.

10A After several weeks at Halton, I passed my trade test and was posted to the KAAP [Kenley Aircraft Acceptance Park] at Kenley Aerodrome, situated between Caterham and Whyteleafe, Surrey. We spent our first few weeks under canvas, adjacent to an American Air Force camp; during that period the permanent hangars, workshops and living quarters had not been completed. My rank at that time was 2nd Class Air Mechanic, Royal Flying Corps.

On completion of the buildings, we were promptly appointed to our quarters and I was soon again involved in the mechanical environment that had been my guiding influence. We were chosen in pairs, our task being to fit the various engines to the numerous bare fuselages that were beginning to arrive at the aerodrome. Some of the early issues were the Armstrong-Whitworth planes to which the 6 cylinder 160hp Beardmore water-cooled engine was fitted. We had to install similar engines in the FE 2B which, unlike, the Armstrong-Whitworth, was a pusher type plane, not a tractor. One of the popular planes during that early period was the RE8. This was powered by the 140hp V8 RAF air-cooled engine. As all these engines had to be started by hand-swinging the propeller, we soon came up against the problem of starting the RE8 engine, on account of the angle of its four-bladed propeller and its height from the ground. For safety, a chain of four people were engaged to pull clear the chap who swung the propeller as soon as the engine fired and started.

10B Here is the 120hp Beardmore engine with its 130mm bore and 175mm stroke. Maximum rpm was 1200; the six cylinders in line were cast separately and surrounded by an electrically deposited copper water jacket. Two sparking plugs per cylinder were used more or less to facilitate starting by the pilot from the cockpit. The combustion head housed two inclined valves, pushrod-operated, the valves being returned to their seats by means of a laminated spring. Very reminiscent of the late Parry Thomas' actuation on the valve gear of many of his racing cars. The crowns of the pistons were concave.

The 90hp Beardmore engine with a bore of 120mm and stroke of 140mm was designed with the same features as the 120hp version. These engines were used to power the larger twin seat biplanes, in particular the Armstrong-Whitworth.

11A Possibly one of the earliest types of plane I was to work on was the Avro biplane, which was, at that time, being used extensively as a training machine. The power unit, an 80hp Gnome rotary engine was something quite new to me and, at the time, had me rather worried. However, Flight Sergeant Eastleigh's tuition and a pile of literature did a great deal to speed up the technique and know-how of the task. Being an air-cooled engine, the water-cooling pipes and ducts used on the orthodox stationary engines were non-existent. Even an exhaust pipe was not needed. Several other more powerful rotary engines were to follow: the Clerget, Le Rhône, Monosoupape, to name just three. These were fitted to the Sopwith Camel and Pup. Not unlike the Armstrong-Whitworth planes, the Avro would practically stall, and more or less remain stationary against a strong headwind. Later, these were superseded by the more rapid DH9, powered by the 160hp Siddeley Puma, and subsequently the DH9A, using the 400hp Liberty engine, as was later used by Parry Thomas in his ill-fated car, *Babs*.

I remember fitting the 150hp Hispano Suiza engine to the SE5 and Sopwith Dolphins. Here again, the engine of this type powered Alistair Miller and Kaye Don's Wolseley Viper at Brooklands during the early post-war years.

11B The Gnome rotary engine was used extensively during the early stages of the 1914-1918 World War. The early type had 7 cylinders of 105mm bore and 140mm stroke and developed 80hp at 1200 rpm. The later type had 9 cylinders and developed 100hp at 1200 rpm with 100mm bore and 150mm stroke. On reflection, I think the later type was known as Le Rhône. They were used to power the Avro biplane, the Sopwith Pup and Sopwith Camel.

12 I was demobbed from the then RAF in 1919 and promptly rejoined Giulio Foresti. My first job was to help him dismantle the engine of a very old, chain-driven 90hp Austro-Daimler, which he intended to race at Brooklands. This old racing car, of unknown origin, had four enormous cylinders with a capacity of 90266cc. I do not recall the bore and stroke, but it was possible to remove the con rods through the apertures in the top of the crankcase after the cylinder blocks had been removed [2 off]. Four automatic inlet valves were housed in cast iron pockets, bolted to the head of the cylinder block, directly over the four exhaust valves which were operated from an orthodox camshaft with exposed timing wheels protruding from the front end of the crankcase.

The teeth on these timing wheels were badly damaged due to stones that had been thrown up by the front wheels and been caught up in the mesh. I was instructed to remove the more damaged teeth and replace these by steel studs tapped and screwed into the timing wheels and then file them to the contour of the existing teeth. This photograph shows the Austro-Daimler at Southend.

13 Foresti entered the 90hp Austro-Daimler for three races in the third Summer Meeting at Brooklands Track where a car of similar appearance, a 110hp Mercedes, was driven by Count Louis Zborowski. In the 100 mph Short we came in second to Malcolm Campbell in his Grand Prix Peugeot, but managed to pass Hawkes in *Vieux Charles*, the Lorraine Dietrich. *Vieux Charles* was, at one time, owned by Campbell and called *Bluebird*. We managed to have an easy win in the 19th 100 mph Long, giving Campbell quite a run with his Peugeot. Another contestant, Geach, driving a 6 cylinder 4 litre Sunbeam, lost control and went off the track near the Sewage Farm. Our average speed was 89¼ mph. The last race over a distance of 2 miles was won by Archie Frazer-Nash with his GN. Pre-handicapped, the Austro-Daimler could not make it in the short distance. Here is the Austro-Daimler in Brooklands Paddock, just after winning the 19th 100 mph Long Handicap.

14 Foresti left England for Monte Carlo early in 1920, revoking his concessions for the Itala, Diatto and Isotta-Fraschini car agencies for the more lucrative challenge of racing cars for some Continental organisations. In his particular way of expressing himself in doggerel English, he said, 'Veela, you wanta come with me to Monaco? I think we go to Sicilia to race in the Targa Florio'.

I needed little persuasion, and after completing the many formalities that were required at that period to obtain a passport, I left Victoria Station on 9th March 1921 and was met by Foresti at Monte Carlo Station the following day. We left for the Itala factory in Torino, travelling by road. I soon learnt that Foresti had been engaged to drive one of the 3 litre Itala cars entered for the XII Targa Florio race on 29th March, but that owing to the political situation and the unrest caused by *Il Duce*, Benito Mussolini, work at the Itala factory had come to a standstill. A small band of enthusiastic mechanics were able to carry on with the completion of the racing cars - using a little bribery, or gaining access via a back wall at the rear of the factory - as we did! But after innumerable setbacks we made it, and were in place on the *traguardo* [starting line] at the appointed time.

ROAD RACING WITH FORESTI

Motor racing in the early twenties was a gripping sport - especially the Targa Florio, where a crash or breakdown in the mountains might leave you at the mercy of bandits! Giulio Foresti and Leo Villa avoided this fate and had successful runs in both Itala and Ballot cars - so successful, in fact, that Capt Campbell took on the British agency for the marques - as well as Leo Villa as his Racing Mechanic.

15 A good picture of Foresti and myself on the line, waiting to take our places for the start. His casual attire made him a great favourite with the crowd. The flower in his mouth was given him by one of his admiring signorinas. Note the steel studded rear tyres which, although they made the distance without a change, did cause me a great deal of anxiety when Foresti applied the footbrake too brusquely on some of the more acute corners.

16 The Targa Florio is known to be the toughest race of them all. Following the First World War, the road was in a very poor state, apart from the undulating road, the surface was covered with loose stones and dust. Four laps of 108 kilometres each had to be covered with treacherous corners and bends. The only time direct gear could be used was a stretch of road 8 km long after leaving Campo Felice.

The 3 litre Itala was a production car, 4 cylinders with side valves. Transmission was through a four-speed [crash] gearbox via a Hele Shaw wetplate clutch, and a live axle with open propeller shaft. The transmission brake was foot operated, the brake drum being situated at the rear of the gearbox. The hand brake operated on two drums with internal expanding shoes on the rear wheels. Suspension was by semi-elliptic leaf springs all round. A single Solex carburettor was fitted, and standard wet sump with spur gear pump was the source of lubrication.

The two other Italian drivers engaged were Moriondo and the works technical engineer, Landi.

Here is a map of the Targa course, otherwise known as the *Circuito delle Madonie* - or Circuit of the Madonnas.

17 With hope and expectancy, Foresti gets underway, having laid a small revolver under the squab of his seat - a precaution many of the other drivers had taken, to combat any unforeseen incidents that might occur in the more isolated parts of the mountains where bandits could waylay and rob any unsuspecting victim. Apart from bandits, my concern was with what might happen if the ruddy thing fired spontaneously due to the jolting over the bumpy road. Safety belts were unknown in those days and on more than one occasion my bottom lost contact with the seat.

18 Apart from one or two almighty skids, we survived two laps and came in to refuel, etc. As we came to a standstill in the pit area, a crowd of Foresti's friends and other enthusiasts descended on the car, excitedly shouting in anything but an orderly fashion. The two front tyres were looking the worse for wear and I leapt from the car and made a dash for the quick-lift jack. But an excitable Italian, wearing an armband and smelling strongly of garlic, got there first and in the scramble to hold onto the jack, I was jostled and finished up on my backside at the back of the pit.

I vaguely remember Foresti, who was standing in the car, shouting out something about, 'Benzina, Presto! Presto!' - or something like that and the radiator cap being unscrewed by some clot, who dropped it on the ground and subsequently doused the bods changing the front tyres with water from an oversized bidon he was using to top up the radiator.

Chaos reigned supreme, but somehow or other the front wheels were changed, petrol tank and radiator caps screwed home and, with many eager hands ready to push-start the car, we left the pits and with shouts of 'Brava! Brava!', were on our way again.

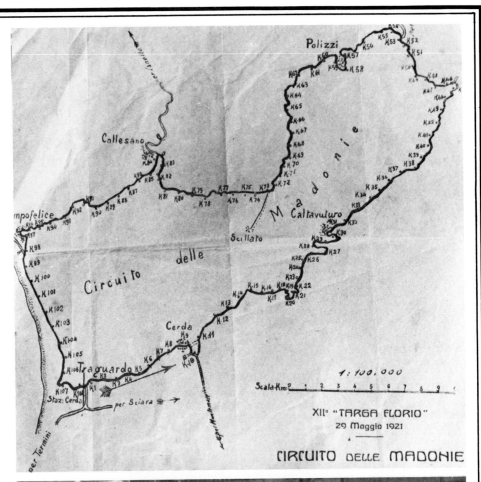

XII° "TARGA FLORIO"
29 Maggio 1921

CIRCUITO DELLE MADONIE

19 We covered the last two laps without
incident, but it was obvious that the race had
taken its toll by the number of *en-panne* and
crashed cars by the roadside. The dust when
overtaking was quite a hair-raising experience
as one's vision was reduced to nil. But we
made it. Tired and weary, maybe, but we had
come in first for the 3 litre Class.

Here is Vincenzo Florio [with hat], the
founder of the race and one of the old racing
drivers, congratulating Foresti on his performance. My reward was 1000 Italian lire and a
rather elegant silver medal. It was a grand
experience and worth all the physical aches
and pains which inevitably followed the
pounding we had received.

20 Following our victory in the 1921 Targa
Florio, Foresti was invited by the Ballot
Brothers to Paris, where two 2-litre sports cars
were being prepared for the 1922 Targo
Florio. His team mate was to be the well-
known French ace, Jules Goux. I was engaged
to help prepare the car and again act as
Foresti's riding mechanic. The 2 litre Ballot,
designed by Henri, was a very advanced car
with an engine of 2 litres capacity, 4 cylinders,
with twin overhead camshafts. Bore .69.5mm
and 130mm stroke. Carburation was via a
single Claudel Hobson carburettor and the
engine developed 72hp at 4000 rpm. Of

standard production, it was a hand-built car, sporting a 4-speed gearbox, a live axle, a dry leather cone clutch. Suspension fore and aft was by semi-elliptic springs mounting Hartford shock absorbers. By far a more advanced car than the 3 litre Itala, and seeing the car was fitted with four wheel brakes gave me some sense of satisfaction. After several road tests the two cars left Paris by road for Genoa and embarked for Palermo, Sicily. This photograph was taken of us at the Ballot factory; note the ornate walls of the works.

21   On arrival at Palermo we drove the cars to Termini Imerese, where our living quarters and workshed were situated. Foresti insisted on decorating his car with a string of bells and coloured ribbons, in fond imitation of the Sicilian mule carts; this move most certainly made him a hot favourite with the Sicilian folk, who showed little respect for some of the German contestants. The decorated bung on the scuttle is the oil tank filler cap. This was Foresti's idea and my job was to replenish the engine oil from cans while underway. The arrangement was not entirely successful on account of the combination of Foresti's haste and the rough state of the road. It misfired on the first attempt and we both received a liberal dose of castor oil - full in the face!

22 Once again we were lined up, awaiting our call to the Starting Line. Foresti, for this occasion, wore a jacket and a cap. Little had changed since the previous year; dust and loose stones still littered the rough road and the six-shooter was again stashed away under Foresti's seat squab. On the advantageous side, we had a fast car well in advance of its time, equipped with four wheel brakes and at least we were not using steel studded tyres.

Foresti not wishing to experience the chaos of the previous year's pit stop, explained that he would have the spare fuel, tyres, etc, left at an undisclosed place in the mountains. To quote his words; 'Veela, we stoppa in de mountain for de benzina and changea de ruote [wheels]. I no wanta de fuss likea de Itala'.

24 By the time we started on our last lap I must have looked a nervous wreck. I felt like one anyway. Foresti, in blissful ignorance of what had happened when we stopped to

23 Foresti made an excellent getaway and when about halfway round on the first lap, he nudged me and excitedly pointed to a clear patch by the side of the road with a clump of bushes in the background. The penny dropped when I realised this was the spot where our petrol, etc, was hidden.

We stopped to refuel at the beginning of the third lap. But somehow his scheme for refuelling did not work out, or possibly I was

at fault. Foresti had arranged for an oversize funnel to be made up, capable of holding the complete 20 litre bidon of petrol. He made it quite clear that I was to jump out of the car, grab the funnel and the bidon of fuel, and actually return and fill the car while underway if necessary, slinging the two surplus items to the side of the road when completed. He would attend to the tyres and remove the petrol tank filler cap.

I think the scheme might well have worked had Foresti got underway with a little more decorum. As it was, he accelerated away violently, causing me to reel backwards against the funnel, which snapped off at the neck, which in turn disappeared into the petrol tank, the body of the funnel, complete with the bidon of petrol, rolling down the spare wheels onto the road.

refuel, was driving like one possessed. We had overtaken a number of cars but I sensed his one ambition was to overtake Jules Goux. I sat there, anticipating the agonising pop back down the induction pipe that invariably heralds a shortage of fuel through one reason or other. We managed to make Campo Felice and, going like hell down the 8 kilo stretch, Foresti hit the culvert running across part of the road that had been constructed as a land drain, with an almighty wallop. The car was practically airborne for a few feet and then hit the road with some force. The impact snapped the leather strap holding the spare wheels and one of the wheels fell off and went rolling down the road. I managed to wriggle round in my seat and grab the end of the trailing strap and pull it over the remaining spare wheel before it joined its counterpart, now lying in the road or bushes. By the grace of God, we made the finishing line to learn that the outright winner of the race had been Count Masetti, driving a Mercedes.

25 In order to gain the maximum publicity for their 2 litre sports car, the Ballot Brothers, Maurice and Albert, insisted that Goux and Foresti should drive the cars back from Genoa to Paris, the two drivers taking different routes. Our return home was not without incident. We developed a bad radiator leak near Rome and had to be towed to a garage to have this repaired. To make matters worse, I developed some tummy pains, the rough roads adding to my discomfort. Foresti was concerned and decided to take me to a hospital when we reached Pisa. In some extraordinary way, the thought of a hospital scared me and scared the pains away, too. He subsequently met Goux in Monte Carlo and we completed our journey to Paris together. Here we are, making our rather triumphant drive down the Champs Elysées to the Ballot Showrooms, which were originally used by Rolls-Royce.

XO·3716

26 On arrival at the showrooms, a large crowd had gathered to receive us. The patron beamed and we were toasted with champagne and surrounded by bouquets of flowers. The Press were there in force and all the headaches and worries we had gone through now seemed worthwhile.

On reflection, the performance of the two cars was remarkable and a tribute to Henri, their designer.

Count Masetti, who won the race, was driving a car which developed twice the horsepower of the Ballot - over 4 litres, I think it was. Goux came in second, his time being 6 hours 52 seconds, just 2 minutes after Masetti. Goux unfortunately skidded off the road into a ditch and he and his mechanic, Pierre du Cros, lost valuable time getting the car back on the road again. In all probability he would have won had this not happened. Foresti came in third, not far behind.

---

27 1923 was to be a year with many surprises. One in particular was when Foresti told me that Malcolm Campbell had taken over the concession for the Itala cars and then Ballot. In order to enhance sales in the UK, Campbell had purchased Foresti's Targa Florio Itala and one of the 3 litre Straight Eight Ballots. Being a shrewd businessman, Campbell realised the publicity to be gained by racing these cars at Brooklands could be a considerable asset.

I was detailed to drive one of the cars to Campbell's home at Povey Cross, near Horley, Surrey, and to assist Foresti in tuning the two cars before handing them over to Campbell.

We left Paris early one morning for Boulogne and eventually, after a pleasant crossing, were met by Campbell at Folkestone. We arrived at Povey Cross late that afternoon, and after parking the cars, Campbell conducted us on a tour of his workshop. Formerly this had been a very old cowshed, but now as a workshop it lacked nothing - one long bench running the full length of the shop, on which was laid out every conceivable tool that one could wish for. An essence of tidiness prevailed and Campbell took the trouble to remind Foresti that this was how he wanted his workshop kept - spick and span.

---

28 Mrs Campbell had arranged accommodation for Foresti and myself and for the first time in my life I was to enjoy the luxury of

sleeping in a fourposter bed. Foresti occupied the bedroom adjacent to my own, but whereas he enjoyed the glorification of taking his meals with the family, I was allocated to take mine with the cook and housemaid in the kitchen.

Like his workshop, the interior of the house was the essence of tidiness. The house was over 500 years old, with its original oak beams and open fireplaces. Campbell favoured the old days and was attracted to anything antiquated. He had gone to a great deal of trouble and expense to furnish the house to suit the period when the house was constructed, and had succeeded to the extent that one could visualise old menfolk trotting around in knee breeches and wearing tricorn hats. The morning following our arrival at Povey, Campbell pushed off to his showrooms in Albemarle Street, London, leaving Foresti

and I to sort out the Itala and the 3 litre Ballot.

Foresti's comments to me in the workshop later were, 'My God, Veela, dis chap Capitano Campbell is extraordinario, he must hava plenty of *soldi* [money], yes!!'

---

29   I was soon to learn that Campbell was an exacting type of person who considered nothing was impossible. He was certainly a most capable and fearless driver and, at the time, gave me the impression of being a brilliant theorist, despite an inclination to be suspicious.

Foresti and I had a good look over Campbell's old Peugeot that was parked in the workshop. This was the car that won the 1912 Grand Prix in the hands of Boillot. Campbell

had won a number of races in this old car [the photograph shows them after winning the 33rd 100 mph Short Handicap at an average 92¼ mph], but had now sold it to a Mrs Menzies.

'You remember dissa car, Veela?' Foresti remarked. 'De Capitano multo cross when de Owstro-Daimler pass him lika diss!' and he gesticulated with his hands whilst emitting a swishing sound with his mouth. My mind went back to my first races with Foresti at Brooklands. Taking a closer look at the Peugeot engine, one could see the hallmark of the brilliant designer who had created those Ballot sports cars - Henri, no less.

Campbell returned that afternoon with one of the 2 litre Ballots, which he wanted us to hot up for him as he had entered it for a race at Brooklands.

30 'Here is the 2 litre Ballot with Foresti as passenger, after winning the 90 mph Short Handicap. Leslie Callaghan of Shell Oil is leaning on the car's tail.

As Campbell wished to race the 3 litre Itala as a standard sports model, the car was taken to Jarvis & Co, the Coachbuilders at Wimbledon, where an orthodox 2 seater body, with dicky, was designed and fitted to it, replacing the body with the saddle petrol tank as was fitted for the Targa Florio.

The 2 litre Ballot was successful when it made its debut a Brooklands for the 90 mph Short, lapping at 89 mph. We did not do so well with the 3 litre Ballot. At the August Meeting, the sluggishness in getting away, due to the limitations of slipping the dry-cone clutch and the poor performance of the two large choke Claudel Hobson carburettors when accelerating, did not go hand in hand with Campbell's fiery temperament.

Campbell had hinted that he would be quite prepared to give me a permanent situation as his racing mechanic should I wish to join him, and some time later, when our return to Paris was contemplated, Foresti again mentioned the subject. Although I did find Campbell rather exacting and demanding in many ways, his personality did counterbalance many of his harsher points. I thought of the comforts of that fourposter as opposed to the dreary bedroom at the Riff Hotel in Paris, and the opportunity of getting home to be with my parents again. So I decided to stay. Foresti's words when he left for Paris were, 'My God, Veela, you gotta some job, old sportie!'

WITH CAMPBELL ON TRACK & BEACH

**Working for the fastidious Capt Campbell kept Leo Villa occupied
at all hours of the day and night.
There were customers' cars to be serviced, new cars to be checked over
and Campbell's growing stable to be tuned and cosseted.
Every week saw preparations for a hill climb, speed trial or race on beach or circuit
and, as if that was not enough, Campbell began to take a serious interest
in capturing the World Land Speed Record as well.**

31   I did quite a lot of work on the 3 litre Itala, but achieved little to enhance its speed without running into problems with a new type of magnesium piston that I experimented with.

I spent many an evening in Campbell's study where I learnt quite a lot about his past racing career and, surprisingly, that he was keen to purchase the 350hp Sunbeam which,

at that time, held the Land Speed Record of 129.7 mph, in the hands of Kenelm Lee Guinness on Brooklands Track. Campbell assured me that he himself had reached a speed of 135 mph on Saltburn Sands, Yorkshire, [the photograph shows him at the time of this run] before I joined him.

'Believe me, Villa, that car is bloody fast and I intend to get it.'

The persistence of Campbell was incredible. One Saturday morning, the 350 Sunbeam arrived at Horley Station. Hasty preparations were made to tow the car back to Povey, but Campbell decided otherwise. The engine was started and Campbell drove the car down to Burtenshaws, the coachbuilders in Reigate, for a re-paint and adjustments to the seat. That run to Reigate was not without incident;

although Campbell got quite a kick out of it, he afterwards stated,

'I very much doubt if anybody will ever cover that 5 miles as quickly as I have just done!'

However, a damaged gearbox, and the sheared driving shaft of the scavenging oil pump on the engine, were to cause us some anxiety and concern.

32 I was not altogether surprised when Campbell told me that he had made a deal with Louis Coatalen and had purchased the 6 cylinder 5 litre Sunbeam, in addition to the 350hp car. Campbell had, on more than one occasion, mentioned his successes in hill climbing events before I joined him. He stated that, apart from the 6 cylinder Sunbeam being a very fast car for Brooklands, it was a similar car that held the record for the Shelsley Walsh Hill Climb, when driven by C A Bird, who made the climb in 52.4 secs. It appears that three of these cars were built secretly by the Sunbeam Company at Wolverhampton during the First World War and would have run in the 1919 Indianapolis 500 Mile Sweepstake, but were not accepted on account of their cylinder capacity being too high. We found the car during our early tests at Brooklands extremely fast, but we did have engine trouble. Nevertheless, the car felt very stable when doing a lap speed in the region of 118 mph. Campbell insisted that he preferred all his racing cars to be hand started when possible, and up to that time I had managed to accomplish this. But the 6 cylinder car did create problems on account of a sensitive range of the advance and retard control fitted on the steering column. When starting, I starting, I would pre-set the position of the lever, but Campbell took a delight in advancing the lever a notch or two, which would cause the engine to backfire viciously. On one occasion this happened and my wrist was badly strained. I'm afraid I saw red and bawled out, 'Why the hell don't you leave the damned lever alone!'

To which he replied, 'Don't you bloody well talk to me like that, Villa!'

---

33 Campbell had entered the 350hp Sunbeam for the first post-war International Meeting on Fanö Island in Denmark on 23rd June 1923. The car was returned from the coachbuilders leaving us with a bare three weeks to sort out the damaged gearbox and oil pump. The new pump and drive were easily replaced, but the damaged layshaft, with two of its intermediate gears chewed up, presented problems. I was ably assisted by Harry Leach [who was later to be involved in the R101 disaster at Beauvais, France, and was one of the four survivors who lived to tell what happened]. Campbell, with his usual determination and personality, persuaded Vickers to supply us with a forging in steel for the layshaft, and later had the Sunbeam Motor Co working overtime to do the machining. Even so, with the car shpped aboard the *SS Bernstein*, ready to leave for Esbjerg, it was only by the superhuman effort made by Howard Webster, who was detailed to join us, that the shaft reached us before the boat sailed. On arrival at Fanö, Harry, Webster and myself worked round the clock fitting the new shaft. By midday, 22nd June, we towed the car onto the beach.

34 To our dismay, we found the surface of the sand full of ripples left by the outgoing tide, in addition to which, Campbell was most unhappy about the single rope barrier extended down the course.

However, the engine was warmed up and Campbell got rolling for his first test run. The car was soon out of sight, although the boom from the open exhaust was still audible. Some minutes had elapsed when one of the officials drove up to us and stated that Campbell was in trouble at the far end of the course. We all scrambled into the 17/30 Itala service vehicle and made tracks for the far end of the course, wondering whether that ruddy gearbox had packed up again.

When we arrived where the car had come to a standstill, Campbell was standing by the radiator, a worried look on his face. He came over to us and exclaimed,

'What a bloody ride! This course is impossible. Apart from nearly wrecking the car, I've literally shaken my guts out. I think I've busted something up the front end, I hope it isn't the axle. I doubt if we will ever do any good in this damned place!'

On investigation, we found the complete assembly for the front shock absorber had broken away. With our tails well down, they towed me back to the shed.

---

35 Burning the midnight oil again seemed inevitable. Time was running out. Fortunately, the main chassis was impaired in no way, but although we had spare shock absorbers, we had no spare trunnions which

were mounted to the chassis. Improvisation was the way out and although we found some items that might be used, we were dependent on what Campbell and some of the club officials could find for us. While waiting, we checked the car over and found all was OK. Campbell returned later with a miscellany of bits and pieces and, with the aid of a welding set and a little perseverance, we were able to overcome our problems. We left the shed for a spot of shut-eye about midnight. When we assembled at the shed the following morning,

Campbell told us that some of his opponents had not rated the Sunbeam's chances too highly and had decided to make the event a scratch race in lieu of the handicap system that had originally been intended.

On Saturday, 23rd June, the event for speed trials took place, each competitor being timed separately. Campbell made two runs and clocked an average of 138 mph, hitting a speed of 146 on one of these runs. The photograph shows him doing just that, whilst crossing the Finishing Line. As the timing

apparatus used did not comply with AIACA regulations, this speed was not officially nomologated.

36 The following day, the club ran the scratch race that had been nominated by some of the German contestants who had thought Campbell did not have a chance. The most formidable cars were the 11,150cc Stoewer with its 6 cylinder aero engine to be driven by the German Kordewan [*seen in this photo*], and the four cylinder Opel 10,512cc, which put up the fastest time at Fanö in 1922, to be driven by Carl Jorns.

At the start, when the flag fell, the Sunbeam literally shot away, leaving the Stoewer and Opel standing. Campbell's time for the Standing Mile was 45.3 secs, the Opel 48 secs and the Stoewer 50.25 secs.

We had a jubilant return home, all of us agreeing that our efforts had been well worthwhile. Campbell showed his appreciation by awarding each of the team with a silver cigarette case. The inscription on mine was: 'To Leo Villa. One of the Troops. From the Skipper'.

37 On our return to England, Campbell was told that René Thomas intended to go for the Land Speed Record with a 350hp Delage and that Ernest Eldridge had made some major modifications to his 300hp Fiat *Mephistopheles*, intent on the same purpose. Campbell was not too happy about the stability of the Sunbeam and did think we would have to find more speed if he was to stay in the picture. To make this possible, the car was despatched to

Boulton & Paul to effect a better streamlined body, whilst Harry Leach and myself were detailed to extract more power from the engine when the streamlining had been completed.

In the interim, I was left to work on the 6 cylinder Sunbeam as Campbell had entered it for some speed trials on Porthcawl Sands. Campbell made a test run with the 6 cylinder within a week of our returning to this country, and was successful in making the fastest time of the day, succeeding in breaking the record

for the 1 mile course, which was the limitation of this particular stretch of sand. From a standing start, he clocked 47.25 secs and was doing 110 mph when he passed the winning post. His opponents were those well-known and successful drivers, H W Cook driving his Vauxhall, Lionel Martin driving his Aston Martin and Major Halford and George Eyston. The last race of the day ended in near disaster when Campbell, who was overtaking Cook's Vauxhall, was nearly caught by the waves of an incoming tide.

38 We left Porthcawl the following day to be present at the Caerphilly Hill Climb, organised by the South Wales Automobile Club, who had promoted the event at Porthcawl.

This was to be my first experience of taking part in a hill climb and I was looking forward to the challenge. All of our opponents who had taken part in the event at Porthcawl were present to vie against each other for the honour of being the fastest up this 1 in 6.2 gradient. The total distance was 1,194 yards, incorporating several sharp bends. When our turn came, apart from wheel-spin, Campbell got away well and when we negotiated the bends, I shifted the weight of my body to counteract the tendency for the car to heel over. Campbell was really stepping it up on third gear, but got into a broadside skid on the last left-hand bend.

39 We slid round in a complete circle and found ourselves facing the wrong direction. I have a hazy recollection of the spectators scrambling from the side of the road. I was hanging on like hell, but finished up by sitting on the exhaust pipe and singeing my breeches. I think Campbell muttered something about,

'Sod the thing!'

I was approached by a young spectator who said, 'Gee, you did look scared!' Perhaps I was!

We descended the hill and made another run and received quite a round of applause from the spectators. However, as Campbell had never made an attempt on this hill before, I think he did quite well to bring home a trophy for the fastest time in the Unlimited Class.

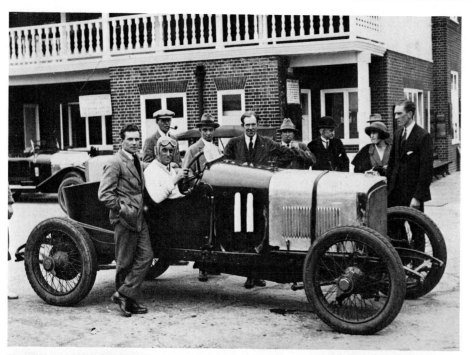

40 Boulton & Paul, who were attending to the modifications of the streamlining for the 350hp Sunbeam, had not yet completed the work, so Campbell entered the Itala in two races for the Autumn Meeting. His main opponent was W O Bentley, who had modified his 3 litre out of all proportion to the standard version. Its wheelbase was reduced to 9ft and the radiator was now considerably lower. It looked like a *pukka* racing car, compared with Campbell's standard sports car, with its two-seater and dicky.

On the line, Campbell was in anything but a good mood and, glaring at me, he muttered, 'I haven't got a bloody hope with this ridiculous handicap'. I did think he had, as the old Itala was going very well. But regrettably, at one point in the race, the Bentley came streaking past us, going very well indeed; Campbell's utterances were drowned by the roar of the exhaust. As we came through the gates, he muttered, 'I told you so'.

However, he received a better handicap in the 90 mph Long Handicap, the last race, and easily came in first. This photograph shows us just outside the clubhouse, after that particular victory, at an average speed of 75.14 mph.

41 I was more than surprised to learn that FIAT of Torino had entered two cars for the JCC 200 Mile Race to be run at Brooklands on 13th October - more so as Campbell had agreed to drive one of them. Much secrecy surrounded these 1½ litre cars, apart from the fact that they were supercharged, this would be something quite new to Brooklands at that period.

The venture was of wholly Italian origin. All those taking part, Campbell excepted, had been works-nominated. Unfortunately, I was to be excluded. I went down to Brooklands on the day of the race and was introduced to my counterpart. I could converse in Italian and, after a brief chat, wished him good luck. But I hated his guts for taking my place!

Much speculation had been placed on the invincible Talbots, which had been entered. After their successes in 1921 and 1922, much was anticipated.

The Talbot team had withdrawn and the odds on the two Fiats having a walkover was more or less a foregone conclusion. Their lap speed during some of the practice runs often reached 101 mph. Knowing Campbell was a man who, all being well, would not accept being second, I backed him for a quid with Long Tom, the well-known Brooklands bookie. The Fiats weighed a little in excess of 10 cwt and developed 80 bhp; 4 cylinders with twin overhead camshafts; the bore and stroke was 65mm x 112mm; a Roots type blower was used. At the conclusion of the 1100cc Class Race, won by Bueno driving a Salmson, the two Fiats left the Paddock for the Fork. Salamano, the Fiat No 1 driver, had driven on Brooklands before and hoped to crack some of the 1500cc Class records during the race. The cars moved up to the Starting Line and Ebblewhite made to gain control, holding up his flag.

42 Ebblewhite's flag fell and amid a deafening noise and clouds of smoke, the race started. I fully expected to see Malcolm first through the haze and was surprised to see that Leon Cushman's Bugatti had taken the lead, followed by an Aston Martin and then the Alvis driven by Harvey. Through Lap One, Cushman held the lead with Salamano and

Campbell hot on his tail. But on the second lap, Salamano took the lead, with Campbell close behind. The silence of the two Fiats as they sped their way round the concrete saucer was apt to give a false impression of the speeds they were attaining. With regular monotony they sped on, increasing the gap between themselves and the cars behind. I think it was on the ninth lap that Campbell took the lead from Salamano. This I had anticipated. The order then was Campbell, Salamano, Eyston on an Aston Martin, Harvey's Alvis and Cushman's Bugatti.

On the thirteenth lap, Salamano came off the Byfleet Banking - as you can see - with smoke streaming from under the scuttle dash. He was unable to make his pit on account of the cars following, so he pulled up on the other side of the track, just short of his pit. When the car came to a standstill, tongues of flame appeared through the bonnet louvres. Some extinguishers were rushed from the pits to quickly put out the flames, once the track was clear. After a hasty conference with his manager, Fiat No 1 was declared retired.

43 Campbell now had a commanding lead, but on the 15th lap, he went missing and after some minutes cruised into the pit with a dead engine. Campbell excitedly exclaimed, 'The engine was getting very hot and losing power, so I switched off'.

After some subdued talking by the Fiat officials, Campbell was urged to try and keep running. 'I'll probably wreck the engine,' Campbell commented. But several of the Italians bawled out, 'Via! Via! Presto! Presto!' and Campbell's mechanic energetically gyrated the starting handle. The engine responded half-heartedly and when Campbell increased the rpm, some unholy mechanical noises were heard. Campbell switched off and raising his arms in a gesture of despair, bawled out, 'Finito!'.

The dominating Fiats were out, and the race was won by Harvey driving the Alvis with an average of 93.29 mph. This photograph shows just that scene, with Hugh McConnell, the well-known Brooklands scrutineer, looking on.

44 The Sunbeam was returned to the works for some modifications. I was fortunate to be given the opportunity of driving the car up to Wolverhampton, and had a great run, but regrettably was pulled up by the police before I reached Stony Stratford, after having a dust-up with a works Bentley in chassis form. Possibly I did not make my plight any easier when I asked the cops to give me a push start, purposely leaving the switch off for quite some distance. Switching on was heralded by a terrific bang down the exhaust pipe and, glancing back, I saw one of the cops sprawling on his backside in the road. The 6 cylinder was later driven direct to Shelsley Walsh by Perkins, the well-known Sunbeam racing specialist. Campbell made the journey by road with Mrs Campbell. I had to go to London to work on one of his customer's Italas.

Although Campbell made the fastest time for the Unlimited Class, with 54.85 secs, Raymond Mays on a Brescia-type Bugatti did a run in 52.8 secs. Malcolm's second run recorded 51.9 secs in the team event, but as only the first run counted, Bird's old record of 52.4 secs still stood.

45　The 350 Sunbeam was returned to Povey Cross just before the close of 1923. At that period, a number of 2 litre Itala chassis had arrived from the works at Torino and Campbell had rented two lock-up garages in Rodmarton Mews at the back of Baker Street to deal with these. I was detailed to check these chassis over, have tyres fitted, tune and test them, before their despatch to the coach-builders, where bodies were constructed and fitted to them. I did find working on these side valve, 4 cylinder engines quite tame, after the more sophisticated 8 cylinder Ballot and the 6 cylinder Indianapolis Sunbeam. I did, however, enjoy testing these cars, using Foresti's old test hill, Fitzjohn's Avenue in Hampstead.

I was joined by Harry Leach early in the New Year, and we returned to Povey Cross in an endeavour to increase the hp of the 350 Sunbeam.

The cylinders were removed, valves ground in and a new set of pistons, giving a slightly increased compression ratio, fitted. Harry had made a study of the two carburettor air intakes and had designed a single balanced intake with the main air entry placed directly behind the radiator. His idea was to promote a ram effect at speed. Unlike last year, when we were working against the clock to have the car ready for Fanö, the work was carried out without haste and the car was afterwards transported to Jarvis, the coachbuilders at Wimbledon, to have the rest of the bodywork completed and painted. Here it is, outside Jarvis, being loaded for departure, your humble servant sitting in the cockpit.

46　Campbell's premonition that the Land Speed Record would be raised before he made another attempt proved correct. In July 1924 Ernest Eldridge, driving his Fiat-engined *Mephistopheles* at Arpajon, France, created an official record of 146.01 mph. By early August that year we were making some trial runs on the beach at Fanö. To compete in some of the Limited classes, Campbell had taken the 6 cylinder Indy Sunbeam over to give some of the smaller GP cars a run for their money.

The atmosphere was very much that of the previous year and despite Campbell's warning the single rope each side of the course was still used to keep the spectators back.

Leslie Callaghan from Shell-Mex was with us and Bill Marshall, John Cameron, Captain Leper - all Campbell's friends - were there to help. The team - Harry, Webby, myself and an ex-boxer [for security reasons] - made up the working party, all of us being presented with woollen sweaters and hats, on which was woven, back and front, the Union Jack. This was, without doubt, a 100% British effort.

47　Although we experienced no major mechanical problems, Campbell was inclined to be disappointed with the 350 Sunbeam's performance, apparently all the thought and work Harry and I had put into the modifications to the power unit had not enhanced the car's maximum speed by overmuch. On the other hand, the modifications to the body, according to Campbell, had most certainly improved the car's stability.

The balanced air intake had now become suspect, but before making any drastic alterations, it was decided to dispense with the main exhaust pipe and this was cut away, leaving only the short stubs from each cylinder.

48 With John Cameron driving a 17/30 Itala the Sunbeam was towed to the Line for a record run on 24th August. At the time, we were using Englebert beaded edge tyres. Sitting on the rail of the Sunbeam is Captain John Leper, who had joined the Forces with Campbell, way back in 1914.

49 Our hopes ran high when Campbell climbed into the cockpit of the 350 Sunbeam on the morning of the 24th. With the aid of a piece of tube to lengthen the hand-hold on the starting handle, Webby and I cranked the engine over after Campbell had bawled out, 'Contact!' With the engine running, and one and all wishing 'the Skipper', as he now wished to be called, good luck, the all-clear was given and he started on what was hoped to have been a record run.

Tension ran pretty high as we all stood around in silence, after the noise of the booming exhaust had receded in the distance, and after what seemed to be a never-ending spell of anxious moments, a motor cyclist approached us at quite a pace to say that the Sunbeam had developed tyre trouble and had stopped at the end of the course.

Apart from Bill Marshall, who suffered from a deformed leg, we all scrambled into the Itala and drove post haste to the end of the course, where we found the old Sunbeam, her nose pointing seawards, minus her back tyres.

50 With some assistance, the car was pushed back to the centre of the track. Campbell showed some concern and told us he had one hell of a job to keep the car straight, on account of the inner tube from the nearside tyre fouling the brake mechanism and locking the offside wheel.

'It was fantastic to see those two bloody tyres hurtling by me as I grappled to keep the bitch straight,' he exclaimed.

Campbell now had the choice of using the beaded edge tyres for his next run, or changing over and using the wire edged type. Both types, at the speeds we were now attaining, were of an unknown quantity, so Campbell decided to leave the existing tyres on the front wheels, but change over to the wired edge for the rear wheels.

Harry, Webby and I changed the wheels and, after giving the car a thorough check, the engine was re-started and Campbell set out on his second run.

This proved to be disastrous. The car, according to the Skipper, was going like hell when a front tyre blew out and left the wheel. It hurtled towards the crowd and timing box, which it more or less demolished, after having knocked down a small boy spectator.

51 The photographer who took this remarkable shot had no idea that he had the tyre in focus until the film was developed. The young lad, who had the misfortune to get bowled over by the tyre - Master Clausen, aged 13 years - was taken to hospital, but died of internal injuries. This cast a gloom over the enterprise and Campbell was placed under open arrest, pending enquiries; the car was impounded. The officials admitted that Campbell had complained about the marshaling and the organisation in general. Campbell was cleared of all blame and we were allowed to return to England. Campbell never returned to Fanö.

52 We returned to England a very disappointed team, I'm afraid the Skipper the more so on account of the costs of the Fanö endeavour and the knowledge that he had not succeeded in wresting the Land Speed Record [LSR] from Eldridge.

While the 350 Sunbeam now lay dormant at Povey, I worked on the Indy 6 cylinder Sunbeam, which was to be successful in winning the Lightning Short Handicap, lapping at 111.92 mph and averaging 103 mph in the August Meeting, also getting the double with a win in the Lightning Long Handicap with an average of 107.55 mph, lapping at 112.42 mph. In between times, I would be working in the dingy lock-ups in Rodmarton Mews. On one occasion, I was fitting some instruments to the 6 cylinder Sunbeam and, glancing up, saw a rather smartly dressed young lady gazing at me. In the ordinary way, I probably would have passed the incident by, but somehow the smile, and the personality her face expressed, attracted me as never before and I felt compelled to jump out of the car and speak to her. From that time on, Rodmarton Mews to me was a sanctuary. I was to meet her there often. Her name was Joan.

PENDINE

Having captured the LSR by a hairsbreadth in the old Sunbeam
the Skipper turned his attention to a brand new Record car
using the still secret Napier Lion aero engine.
Despite all these activities he still found time to take on Chrysler and Bugatti agencies
and race their wares [suitably modified by Leo] at Brooklands and elsewhere.
The Skipper's cars were now called *Bluebirds* and his determination
to keep the LSR in British hands
meant a hectic time for Leo and weeks of preparation,
often on rain-soaked beaches far from the comforts of Povey Cross.

53 The tyre problems which caused the mishap at Fanö gave the leading tyre manufacturers a great deal to think about and the Dunlop Tyre Co had now produced a new type of wheel rim and tyre, to be known as the well-based type. Campbell's insatiable desire to get that LSR knew no bounds, and during September the Sunbeam was loaded onto a Scammell lorry and transported to Pendine Sands, Carmarthenshire. We had the Dunlop Tyre Co 100% behind us and prospects now looked more hopeful. We did, however, run into trouble on account of cross winds and very wet sands. To prevent the car from sinking axle deep, metal sheets or planks were used. Harry Leach was recalled to Cardington where he was engaged as Chief Engineer on the R101 airship, so Webby and I had to manage the best way we could.

The damp, cold September weather and the soft wet condition of the sand affected the car's performance in no small way and the driving conditions for the Skipper were appalling. On Wednesday, 4th September, Campbell made his first attempt and clocked an average of 146.16 mph, beating Eldridge's record of 146.01 by a mere margin.

54 Many changes and a great deal of action took place during 1925. My working quarters were moved to Sussex Place, South Kensington, where Campbell had opened a first class showroom to deal with his car sales. Complete with underground workshop and hydraulic lift, one section was partitioned off for me to work on his racing cars.

Campbell had decided to try to raise his record with the 350 Sunbeam, and the car was taken back to Jarvis, the coachbuilders, to have the radiator cowl modified and the through exhaust pipes replaced. Harry and I worked on the engine while this improvement was being carried out. We fitted different camshafts and removed the balanced air intake, replacing the two separate vertical intakes. On completion of the task, the Sunbeam was loaded and transported to Pendine.

As Parry Thomas, H O D Segrave and a foreign entrant were now hot on Campbell's tail to create new LSRs, Campbell had decided to have a world beater capable of 180 mph+ designed and constructed.

55 Our second visit to Pendine this time was of some duration as, notwithstanding spells of inactivity on account of winds and rain, Campbell's faith in the old 350 had induced him to enter it for some Standing Start speed events on Skegness Sands. On 8th June he beat all comers, including Parry Thomas' 7.3 litre Leyland Thomas, which was driven by J E P Howey, covering the Standing Kilometre in 33.4 secs [average speed 66.97 mph]. Harry and I had our hands pretty full, but the Skipper boosted our enthusiasm when he remarked that the car felt much livelier now.

Back at Pendine, Campbell entered the 350 for another event, organised by the South Wales Automobile Club; here again, he put up the fastest time of the day, covering the Standing Mile in 38.45 secs [92.78 mph]. Campbell had now acquired the agency for Chrysler cars and had entered a 6 cylinder 3203cc, which won its class with an average speed of 52.64 mph. The Skipper derived much satisfaction in being able to beat one of the works models, driven by Noel Martin, who came in second with a speed of 50.5 mph. I must add that Harry and I burnt a fair amount of midnight oil at Povey, raising the compression ratio and fitting twin carburettors to the Chrysler side valve engine.

56 The very changeable weather conditions and rippled beach prevented any chances of the record attempt. Even on slow trial runs, the wet sand thrown up by the wheels hindered the Skipper's vision; so we made up a windscreen from some brass sheet, using talc as a substitute for glass. Fortunately, the hospitality afforded us by the Ebsworth family, who owned the Beach Hotel, most certainly balanced out the more frustrating and dull periods. Their liberal portions of ham and eggs at breakfast time will remain unforgettable. The main bar room was liberally festooned with whole cured hams - a sight one seldom sees these days. At long last, on the morning of Tuesday, 21st July, the Skipper had driven a car faster than any man alive and was the proud owner of the Fastest Car in the World. His average speed for the two runs was 150.86 mph. On this occasion, we had no tyre trouble and the official RAC timing method was used. It was truly an all-British effort and received a great deal of publicity. The Skipper, his team, and *Bluebird* had generated a lust for ultra high speeds, which was to affect the lives of many of the notable worldwide racing drivers for years to come.

57 Campbell had nurtured the impression that Count Louis Zborowski's Higham Special was intended as a contender for the LSR. In one sense his deductions were correct, but not quite as Campbell had imagined them. The effects of Higham, the Count's estate near Canterbury in Kent, were sold when Zborowski lost his life on the Monza Race Track driving a Mercedes. Parry Thomas purchased the Higham Special for a very moderate sum, made several modifications, and renamed the car *Babs*.

As I have previously mentioned, Campbell's endeavours had whetted the appetite of the more notable Brooklands drivers and Parry was the first to accept the challenge, appearing with *Babs* for some early trials in October at Pendine.

Being of Welsh descent, he most certainly received a big welcome from the local fraternity, but owing to the unfavourable weather, beach conditions and some teething troubles with *Babs*, he returned south with the car, after making one or two short runs. Here is *Babs* in her 1926 form, which Parry gave to her soon after his return from Pendine.

58 Reverting to the earlier period of 1925, I must point out that although my time was occupied with working on the 350 Sunbeam and various other less interesting occupations, to promote the Itala car sales, Campbell had persuaded the Itala Company to loan him one of their competition cars and, in due course, one of the more successful types, the 2.8 litre, was brought to this country by Signor Rebuffo, who had driven it in the 1924 Coppa Florio. This car, apart from a slightly decreased bore and stroke, still retained the side valve monobloc engine configuration with a single carburettor; its all-up weight being somewhat decreased. The car was entered for the Easter Meeting 90 mph Short Handicap, but when leading in the race, it sustained a broken fuel line, rendering it *hors de combat*. Kidstone, driving a 2 litre Bugatti, won.

Later in the day, however, lapping at 81.85 mph in the 90 mph Handicap, the Itala was first to cross the Finishing Line. Here is the traditional victory photo

59 Campbell had reached the conclusion that his 350hp Sunbeam had surpassed its limit and, being a man who never under-estimated his opponents, regarded Parry Thomas' recent trials with *Babs* as a serious challenge. He set in motion an ambition he had for some time, to have a special car constructed - his target 180 mph.

To do this, he engaged Amherst Villiers, the well-known designer, who had been assisting Raymond Mays to increase the performances of his Brescia Bugattis, *Cordon Rouge* and *Cordon Bleu*; both these cars had put up some astounding performances at most of the classic hill climbs.

Reposing on the floor of the workshop at our new showrooms in Sussex Place was a brand new 450hp Napier Lion aero-engine (still on the Secrets List) that Napiers of Acton had loaned to Campbell. Amherst, who was now residing at Povey Cross, was to design a chassis that would accommodate this engine. Having set the wheels in motion, Campbell (an adventurer at heart) set sail on board Kenelm Lee Guinness' yacht, *The Adventuress*, with a small party, for Cocos, a desolate and vermin-infested island, four hundred miles off the coast of Colombia in South America. His quest? Buried treasure!

I was not included in this adventure but returned to Povey Cross, where I dismantled the 3 litre Itala engine for Amherst, who was engaged to design its new camshaft.

60 The first hint I received that Campbell had taken on the agency for the Chrysler Car Co was one evening, when he drove an open four seater Chrysler into the garage at Povey. 'See what you can do with this, Villa, there's a good chap,' he called out as he got out of the car, adding, 'It's supposed to do 70 mph but it's got no bloody guts at all!'

On lifting the bonnet, I found that, although a six cylinder engine, boasting two carburettors and a detachable head, this Chrysler was a side valve unit and I was most disappointed. I spent the next day testing the car on the road, aided by a box of various Solex carburettor jets and a tool bag.

Subsequently, when Campbell tried the car, he remarked, 'Well done, Villa! How did you do it? A remarkable improvement, but she's using far too much petrol, old boy. See what you can do about it'.

I spent a great deal of time on that car, which was to undergo many modifications and, incidentally, to lose one or two races. Finally, after many teething troubles, a higher back axle ratio was fitted and the car taken to Jarvis & Co of Wimbledon to have a special streamlined body fitted.

61 When the Chrysler was completed by the coachbuilders, Campbell lost no time in taking it down to Brooklands for a try-out. I must admit it was a very comfortable ride and although Campbell used some restraint on 'the urge pedal', the car hovered round the 100 mph mark with little effort.

It was entered for the President's Gold Cup, the 35th 75 mph Long Handicap. With the car's previous losses, it would appear that Campbell had built up a reasonable handicap for himself. I fact, barring accidents, his chances of winning the race looked pretty hopeful. So, with his old friend Hoppy Marshall, who had been with us at Fanö, he laid out £100 - to win.

Parry Thomas had entered an unknown quantity called the Thomas Special, but the handicap was in Campbell's favour. Campbell was elated and for once had no complaints to make.

Sitting with Campbell on the Starting Line, waiting for Ebby's flag to fall, finds one with mixed feelings. But on this occasion, I was at ease and brimful of hope. No doubt the Skipper's *joie de vivre* promoted this.

The rpm rose, the rear tyres squealed, and we were off and going like hell. I glanced at

the Skipper, whose usual determined grimace somehow appeared more relaxed. On one of the later laps, I looked over my shoulder and was horrified to see Parry coming from under the Members' Bridge. I tapped the Skipper on the shoulder and then Parry shot past us to win the race. We came in second. I will refrain from mentioning the utterances of Campbell and Thomas when they met in the Paddock later, but would add that they were both hauled before the Stewards for giving incorrect details of their relative speeds!

---

62 Campbell entered the Chrysler for the 90 mph Short Handicap in the Autumn BARC Meeting, which he won, lapping 99.61 mph. He then sold the car and I never saw it again. Incidentally, in the President's Cup Race, the Thomas Special had lapped at 101.23 mph.

During Campbell's absence at Cocos, my everyday routine was subject to many changes. In the first instance, I had purchased a 16H Norton motorcycle from O'Donovan, who had a motorcycle business in Portland Street. This

enabled me to pay frequent visits to my home, in lieu of being stuck at Povey Cross.

More important, I was able to see more of Joan, the young lady I had become acquainted with while working at Rodmarton Mews. We grew immensely fond of each other and with little fuss got married at Brixton Registry Office.

After two days honeymoon, I spent some time at Povey, fitting Amherst Villiers' new camshaft to the Targa Itala. This new camshaft made it possible to dispense with the original type of roller tappet for the more orthodox mushroom type. The valve timing was completely altered, which did, in effect, upset the slow running, but in subsequent tests at Brooklands found the car's all-out performance much improved.

---

63 Campbell's axiom 'Records are made to be broken' was very much in my mind, when I heard that Henry Segrave had created a new LSR of 152.33 mph with a 4 litre 12 cylinder supercharged Sunbeam, designed by

J S Irving; the car was built on GP racing-car lines and looked diminutive by comparison with the 350 Sunbeam and Thomas' chain-driven *Babs* [seen in this picture with 'Dunlop Mac', William Hicks, Jock Pullen and, of course, Parry Thomas at the wheel]. The following month, Thomas took *Babs* to Pendine and raised the LSR to 171.02 mph. By this time, Amherst Villiers had designed the chassis for the new *Bluebird* and this was constructed by Vickers and despatched to the Robinhood Engineering Works in Kingston Vale, along with the 450hp Napier engine.

To add to Campbell's worries, something misfired, and Amherst Villiers terminated his engagement quite abruptly with the Skipper.

Joseph Maina, a very competent designer and engineer, was a friend of my family and was more than interested in Campbell's record endeavours. At the time, he had completed the design of a new type of epicyclic gearbox for its inventor, Foster Brown, Esq, who claimed that, unlike the orthodox crash box of that period, it simplified changing speed.

When I had the opportunity to mention these facts to Campbell, he was more than anxious to meet Foster Brown and Maina, so an appointment was duly arranged.

64 An agreement was reached between Foster Brown and Joseph Maina that, in consideration of Campbell using their gearbox for his next record attempt, they would build him, FOC, a special gearbox for his new *Bluebird*. Also, for a nominal sum, Maina would finish the design that Amherst Villiers had left incomplete. In view of his own record being beaten on two occasions, and knowing that the Sunbeam Motor Co were building Segrave a new 1000hp monster, Campbell expressed dire urgency.

Having now accepted the agency to deal with Ettore Bugatti's products, he was having a workshop built for his needs in the Paddock at Brooklands. Our first delivery from the Bugatti factory at Molsheim was a 2 litre unblown Straight 8. Campbell lost no time in trundling me down to the Track to try the car. I must admit, although a hard ride, the performance was astounding. I thought Campbell was a little ham-handed with the gear shift and dropped an occasional 'h'.

He entered the car for the Surbiton MC 50-Mile Handicap and came through an easy winner from scratch, also shattering the 2 litre Class record in the bargain - his average speed being 108.60 mph. Here he is in the Bug, after winning that race. The racing driver, Kaye Don, can be seen on the extreme left.

65 The construction of the Napier-Campbell *Bluebird* - the very focus of the Skipper's hopes and dreams - had now got underway to a good start. Under the supervision of Joseph Maina, many of the Robinhood Engineering staff were engaged to carry out the work, in particular George and Charles Miller, who were later to become part of the *Bluebird* team.

For my part, I was fully occupied, dealing with the different types of Bugattis which

66 An all-out effort was made at the Robinhood Engineering Works [KLG] and when the main part of the work had been completed the car in its unfinished state was transported to Campbell's workshop at Povey Cross. George and Charles Miller had left KLG and were now working for Campbell. Two panel beaters from Jarvis, the coachbuilders, joined us to build the body and Joe Coe from Napiers was the engine specialist. Housing and feeding the team gave Mrs Campbell and her staff some problems, but in those early days, there were no complaints.

My biggest headache was to keep those damned batteries charged up to cope with the electric drills and other mechanised tools that were being used. Just before Christmas, the car was nearly completed and rolled out of the workshop for its first engine run. Like many other designers, Maina had been able to accommodate the petrol tank and other items well within the streamlined shell, and had cut the size of the cockpit down to a bare cut the size of the cockpit down to a bare minimum, so much so that the steering wheel had to be removed to allow Campbell access. He sat in the car for a few minutes, fumbling with the various switches, levers, etc, then exclaimed in a loud voice,

'Bloody marvellous! The biggest car in the world, and I can neither get in nor out of the bloody thing!'

Campbell had entered for many races at Brooklands. After becoming accustomed to working on the more robustly constructed cars like the Sunbeams, etc, I did think - but unjustly so - that the Bugatti structure, particularly round the steering mechanism, could not stand up to the pounding it would receive on the Track.

Initially, we did experience a fair amount of trouble with the Bugatti's aluminium wheels and tyres where, at high speeds, the tyre would creep round the rim, dislodging the valve and deflating the tyre. Subsequently, well-based, spoked wheels were used and apart from an occasional stripped tread, we experienced little trouble.

Although Campbell had many successes with the 2.3 Monoposto Bug, it was a very hard ride and quite a handful. We made him a specially sprung seat, which collapsed when he was testing the car, injuring his spine. He coasted into the Paddock in acute agony. Here is the 2.3 after winning at Brooklands.

67 Without doubt, Campbell's finest effort on Brooklands during 1926 was his performance in the RAC's British Grand Prix. A course was designed with two S-bends in the Finishing Straight, composed of sand bags, one being situated below the Paddock stand, the other just beyond the Paddock.

To do battle, the very successful Straight Eight s/c Delages were to be driven by a team comprising Benoist, Senechal and Wagner, whilst the s/c Talbots were to be driven by Segrave, Divo and Morileau. Campbell had entered one of the latest s/c 1½ litre Straight Eight Bugattis. The car arrived from Strasbourg with a French mechanic, only two days before the race, allowing Campbell little time both for practice and for us thoroughly to check it over.

I was in some doubt as to Campbell's chances agains the invincible Delages and Talbots, when Ebby's flag dropped and I was more than surprised to see Campbell break through and take the lead at the start of the Finishing Straight. The Bug mechanic with me in our pit got really excited when Divo, Segrave and Benoist and Campbell swept through the S-bends in a bunch on the sixth lap. The possibility of Campbell going the distance non-stop raised some doubts, so fuel and re-filling equipment were laid on. Here, towards the end of the race, Senechal overtakes Campbell.

68 The Grand Prix has reached the halfway stage, when misfortune overtakes many of the drivers. The Talbot, driven by Moriceau, retires with a broken front axle in the opening round. The Delage, driven by Wagner, retires with plug trouble on Lap Twelve. Segrave has a burst tyre, losing five minutes, leaving Benoist to gain a two-lap lead. Subsequently, Segrave appears to lose speed and retires. The remaining Talbot, driven by Divo, takes up the challenge and chases the leader, Benoist. Campbell is now lying third after stopping at the pits to take on fuel. Now the leading Delage with Benoist driving pulls into the pits for a tyre change. He is wet through with perspiration from the heat in the cockpit, due to the red hot exhaust pipe running close to the body by the driver's feet; some laps later, he calls into the pits and puts his feet into a bowl of cold water. Subsequently, Senechal pulls into the pits, perspiring and exhausted, to hand over his car to Wagner. Later Benoist, whose feet are severely burned, hands his car over to Dubonnet. Campbell is now in second place and with only three cars left in the race, the result is Senechal and Wagner 1st; Campbell 2nd; Benoist and Dubonnet 3rd.

---

69 It was fortunate that Povey Cross was situated in a more or less isolated spot, otherwise the din through night and day that came from the workshop would not have been tolerated by any near neighbours. The

Crossley generator engine ran incessantly and the log book I was keeping to record its running time was looking somewhat grimy through constant use of dirty paws. The panel-bashers excelled themselves and we were subsequently all suffering from sore throats - the after-effects of shouting when trying to converse. But the work went on unceasingly and Campbell was enjoying every moment of it, buzzing around like a blue-arsed fly, ladling out tins of 50 *Three Castle* cigarettes - pre-war stock, I'm afraid, but very acceptable, nonetheless. His pride and joy - the once-tidy workshop - now looked a shambles, but not a word of complaint was uttered.

Apart from the body to Maina's design, much time was spent making up the various levers and controls, fitting instruments, etc. At Campbell's request, a deadman's switch was fitted to a spoke on the steering wheel, which now had been considerably reduced. This switch in particular was a safety precaution in the event of the throttle jamming open. As the ignition system on the Napier engine comprised two magnetos, the switch gear we made up had its complications. Here is the completed chassis, showing the fuel and oil tank rear and water tank midway on the scuttle.

---

70 As the days went by, so the tempo increased and in more than one instance bouts

of frayed nerves were in evidence. In particular, the extra duties imposed on both the house staff and Mrs Campbell had blunted the keen edge of their enthusiasm of former days. One morning Campbell came into the workshop carrying an armful of neckties; depositing these on the bench he bawled out, 'Here, you chaps! Sort these out amongst yourselves'. He left the garage and we were soon busy making our choice of ties when he rushed back into the garage and bawled out, 'Come on, you bloody lot of fools, the granary's on fire!' The granary had been specially carpeted and furnished with table and chairs and made into a first class dining room for our use, and it was now an inferno, whilst we were all dashing around with buckets of water. But we could not cope and the place was soon gutted. Apparently, the Valor paraffin oil stove had been overfilled and caught alight.

Campbell now severely rebuked the person who had been attending to the oil stove, possibly further aggravating the situation. From that time on, we were all boarded out and valuable time was lost.

But there came one early misty December morning when the end-product of all our sweat and tears, the Napier-Campbell, was rolled out from the workshop for the first time

71 This photograph shows the completed *Bluebird* and the 2 litre Bugatti sandwiching a 'kiddy car', whose occupant is young Master Donald Campbell, many years later to become my employer.

We had the good fortune to spend Christmas 1926 at home with our wives, but returned to Povey soon after Boxing Day, where the *Bluebird* was loaded onto the old chain-driven Scammell lorry, which then departed on the first leg of its journey to Pendine. The team left for South Wales early on 31st January and spent New Year's Eve at the Beach Hotel, Pendine. Campbell had purchased a new Dodge van for our transport, tools and some spares, whilst I had brought along a portable gramophone and a miniature set of drums and was whooping it up with the locals and the team. Then Campbell arrived and hinted that we were to make an early morning start and should get some rest. We did, however, see the old year out and the new one in before 'lights out'.

By Monday, 2nd January 1927, the car was towed onto the soggy, wet beach and the engine started. But trouble with the clutch prevented the Skipper from getting underway. The car started to sink in the soft sands only to be hastily towed from the beach, aided by many of the disappointed spectators who had come down to see the *Bluebird* running.

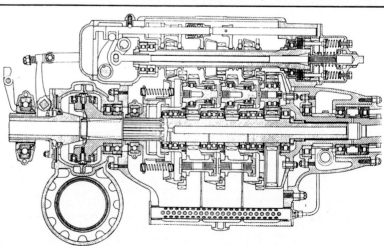

72 Cross winds and mechanical troubles gave Campbell much to think about. The major mechanical trouble was brought about by the malfunctioning of Maina's clutch and gearbox. Apart from the awkward position of the gearbox and its change speed lever situated between Campbell's legs, the Skipper found it impossible to change speed once the car got going. He did manage to get one timed run-in at 133 mph but stalled and had to be towed back to base. Maina's explanation of what the fault was fell on deaf ears, and the car was loaded and returned to Povey. Here, by the way, is the general arrangement of that FBM epicyclic gearbox.

73 Incidentally, Parry Thomas, who at the time held the Record, had paid us a visit at Pendine. Obviously very interested, he is seen here, looking over Joseph Maina's [in cap and scarf] shoulder. Campbell is not looking any too cheerful.

On arrival back at Povey, the gearbox and clutch were removed from the chassis and returned to Messrs Beard & Fitch Ltd of Clerkenwell, who had virtually manufactured the whole of the transmission gear. Joe Coe from Napiers came down and we helped him to fit a new set of higher compression ratio pistons, which I think boosted the hp from its nominal 450hp to in excess of 500hp. It would appear that the Skipper had some doubts as to the nominal 450hp being sufficient.

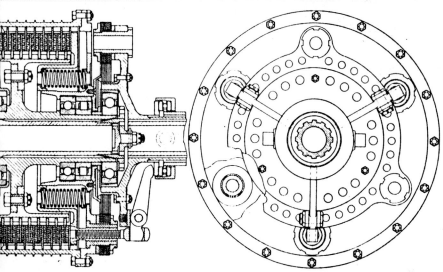

74 Here is the general arrangement of the clutch, showing its unusual features.

Within the fortnight, we were back at Pendine. It had not been possible to road-test the car before we left, but we did manage an engine run, and with the rear wheels lifted clear of the ground, were able to test the gearbox, clutch, etc. Apart from a few minor adjustments, the situation looked promising. When we arrived at Pendine, it was raining and the sodden beach looked more uninviting than ever.

During the following days, the Skipper managed to get some runs in, mostly on a wet beach. He suffered one or two almighty skids due to cross winds and loss of adhesion. On one occasion he went broadside on into the row of marker flagpoles, one apparently missing his head by a narrow margin and putting some sizeable dents in the cowling round the radiator. Nevertheless, the runs that were possible now did prove that the clutch and gearbox were working well.

Although he made some official timed runs, Parry Thomas' record of 172.6 still eluded him. The Skipper's best so far had been 167 and 169 mph; Parry Thomas' time was 13.080 secs, Campbell's best 13.372 secs. To see the difference, just look at the second hand of your own watch or clock!

75 Winds, adverse tides and a waterlogged beach persisted through January 1927. On 1st February, Campbell had the timekeepers at their posts, his intention being to have a go - come what may. On the outward run he clocked 171 mph, but on the return run he was going very fast when the nearside rear tyre burst. He managed to hold the car and returned to base on a flat tyre - as you can see from this photo.

The following day, the local schoolchildren were busy on the beach collecting the numerous shells left by the receding tide, which had caused Campbell's burst tyre on the previous day. In addition to this, Campbell hit upon the idea of ploughing two furrows 50 yards apart, down the 7-mile course, to drain the sea water away. This, however, made things worse. It did dry up the section close to the furrows, but appeared to make the condition midway between the furrows worse - so this idea was abandoned. Many of the locals had also protested against this manoeuvre, hinting that it would permanently ruin their wonderful beach.

76 The Dodge van was used to tow the plough and I must give the Skipper full marks for the way he handled that plough. I was walking alongside while he was operating the thing, when the Skipper bawled out, 'Come on, Villa! You have a go.' I'm afraid my efforts did not amount to much. Somehow I could not manage to hold the share in the sand, try as I might, even with Campbell's advice, and it persisted in coming to the surface. Eventually, it slewed round and knocked me over and I finished with a damaged wrist, tied up with my handkerchief.

77 To counter the liberal amount of salt water thrown up by the front wheels that was finding its way into the cockpit, we made up and fitted two light deflectors which, in a small way, did add to the Skipper's comfort. Our major mechanical problems appeared to

be things of the past. The trusty Napier engine gave us no trouble at all. We were to spend much of our time preserving the exposed bright steel parts of the car from corrosion, following the liberal dowsing with sea water and sand to which the car was subjected. Climatic conditions over which we had no control dictated events. The delays and fees of the timekeepers were costing the Skipper a packet, but he was a determined man and was bent on getting his record back at all costs.

78 On 4th February the wind had dropped, but there were still pools of water on the course. The timekeeprs had been alerted and *Bluebird*, with her attendant nursemaids, was poised ready at Dolwen Point. Later, a small Morris two seater, with Campbell at the wheel, drove up after making a survey of the course. The timekeepers had been alerted and

helmet, goggles and gloves, he asked me if the car was ready. Given the OK, he exclaimed, 'OK, chaps, I'll have a go!' In pensive mood, he walked towards *Bluebird* and lifted himself onto the edge of the cockpit; legs dangling, we wiped the soles of his shoes and he took his place behind the steering wheel. On the word 'Contact!', Joe Coe and myself seized the starting handle and cranked the engine. Amidst clouds of belched black smoke, we all pushed him clear of the planks and he was on his way and soon out of sight. Silent, we stood around with varying thoughts. Then we heard the boom of the exhaust and *Bluebird* hove into sight on its return run. As she came to a standstill, we ran over to Campbell who, with a broad grin, said, 'I think I've done it! Jolly good show, chaps! What a car! She went beautifully!'

Indeed, he had done it - at 174.88 mph. He had wrested the laurels from Parry Thomas.

79 Parry Thomas had sent Campbell a telegram, congratulating him on his achievement. At the same time, he hinted to the Press that he intended bringing *Babs* to Pendine within a few days to recapture his lost record. Thomas had, in fact, booked the Beach Hotel for 15th February.

Segrave, with 200 mph in his sights, had left for Daytona Beach, Florida, with the now completed 1000hp chain-driven *Slug*. Oddly enough, although Thomas' car was chain-driven, he was heard to remark that he did not fancy Segrave's chances with 1000hp being transmitted through chains, irrespective of the fact that an oil bath totally enclosed the chains on the Sunbeam, unlike *Babs*, where the chains were uncovered .

On 3rd March, in poor health at the time, Thomas, while making a bid to regain his record, was killed when one of those driving chains on *Babs* disintegrated. One end acting like a flail, struck him across the head, killing him instantly.

---

80 Campbell was terribly put out when he heard the sad news of Parry Thomas' disaster, and Henry Segrave, who was on the high seas with the *Slug*, bound for Daytona at the time, was seriously thinking of calling his attempt off. However, he did make some trial runs on the beach when he arrived there and, on 29th March, he became the first man to travel in excess of 200 mph on land, establishing a new World's Record of 203.79 mph. Here is Segrave, standing in front of *Slug* on that Florida beach.

This was a stupendous effort and naturally gave Campbell some cause for anxiety, knowing that he had expended a considerable amount of money on the Napier *Bluebird* which was now, in effect, obsolete.

By contrast, and to keep his mind occupied, he concentrated on the Monoposto Bugatti, now fitted with a 2300 s/c engine, which was very fast but quite a brute to hold. It was entered for the Founder's Cup and Campbell was scratch man, losing by 50 yards after a neck-and-neck effort with Kaye Don in the 5 litre Sunbeam.

But another neck-and-neck struggle with Kaye Don followed and this time Campbell lapped at 118 mph, taking an easy victory in the Lightning Long Handicap.

81 Montagu Stanley Napier had taken a keen interest in the LSR and, fortunately for Campbell, was probably even keener to see a Napier product come to the forefront - as was Campbell's eagerness to wrest that record from Segrave.

After many meetings and discussions, it was decided that *Bluebird*'s structure throughout had a safety margin well in excess of its present performance and the possibility of using the very hush-hush engine that was used in the Supermarine Napier Seaplane, which won the Schneider Trophy Race at Venice during September, became a reality. I was towed from Brooklands to Napiers at Acton, where the work was put in hand immediately.

George Miller and myself were despatched to the Napier works to remove the engine, gearbox and rear axle. A private section of the works had been nominated and, with the assistance of some of the Napier technicians, the installation of the new engine went ahead. In appearance, the exterior of the engine, to all intents and purposes, was little changed from our old 450hp. But the innards were a different story, the 12 cylinders having a bore and stroke of 5½ins x 5-1/8ins and a compression ratio of 10:1. The engine developed 875 bhp with an rpm now increased to 3300, so a higher back-axle ratio had to be machined.

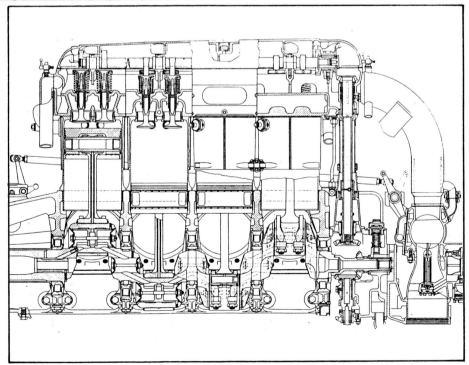

GRAND PRIX
INTERLUDE

Whilst the record-breaking *Bluebird* was re-equipped and re-engined at Napiers,
Campbell and his team were busy racing Bugattis at home and abroad.
Leo recalls the steps he took to ensure that Sabipa could not catch the Skipper
in the French GP and shows us some glimpses of both Campbell and Villa family life,
often disrupted by weeks away from home and much burning of midnight oil.

82 There were many occasions when I would be called away from the tranquil atmosphere of Napiers for the more turbulent tempo of Brooklands to prepare a car for a race that Campbell had entered. In fact, on one occasion, I found myself bound for Boulogne with a 4 cylinder s/c Bugatti and a 2 litre Straight Eight, which Campbell had entered for the French GP and the Georges Boillot Cup. George Miller was with me and we were pushed for time, getting the cars *au point*.

Our chief opponents in the Grand Prix were the French ace, Sabipa, driving a 4 cylinder s/c [the same as Campbell's], and George Eyston driving a 1½ litre Eight. The cars created no problems and Campbell managed to do some fast practice laps. The cars were on the Starting Line with engines running, raring to go, on Saturday, 10th September. It was raining hard and Campbell had made no allowances for this; so I loaned him my short leather coat, which I had just purchased. The starter's flag fell and, with spinning rear wheels, the pack roared off, Sabipa appearing to take the lead. George and myself hastily returned to our pit to deal with any emergency that might occur. We had earlier placed all tools, refuelling equipment, etc, in neat order. Papworth, the Bugatti specialist, was taking care of Sabipa in the adjacent pit.

83 With the rain pelting down, the speakers announced that the leading car had reached Baincthun. We were all on our toes and then the first car, almost obscured by the water thrown up from the road, flashed by. It was the Bugatti driven by Sabipa, who was hotly followed by Campbell in his car, No 48. Rain, wet and a slippery road seemed to present no problems as the two cars flashed by. A rousing cheer went up from Papworth's pit next door, while George and I endeavoured to hide our concern, fumbling with the array of spanners lying on the pit counter.

And with George Eyston now in third place behind Campbell, so that sequence continued. Several cars had slid off the road, while others had mechanical troubles, until the final lap when Sabipa came into his pit with a slipping clutch. Then everything happened. He was yelling out for 'Une broche! Nom de Dieu, une broche!' [small tommy bar]. But this very essential tool was lacking on Papworth's counter and a plea was directed towards us; in the interim, I had knocked that very essential piece of steel onto our pit floor and was standing on it. While this was going on, Campbell sped by, followed by George Eyston. In a frenzy, the unlucky Sabipa, his clutch still slipping, got rolling again.

---

84 So Campbell, after a non-stop run, was first over the Line, followed by the unlucky Sabipa [4 mins afterwards]. Sabipa spared nothing in his endeavours to catch Campbell and did, in fact, pass Eyston just short of the Finishing Line, making him second, with Eyston a close third.

No doubt many will think that my act was unsporting, but my loyalty was to Campbell and, I am sure, had the boot been on the other foot, it is doubtful whether anybody in my position would have acted differently. There was much jubilation after the Skipper's victory, but George and I had our work cut out, preparing our second car, the 2 litre Eight, for the Georges Boillot Cup, which was staged for the following day. This was to be a Handicap Race, based on the weight and estimated speed of the car. Campbell was not happy about the method used, but decided the experience might be worthwhile!

George and I were supplied with liberal amounts of wine whilst working on the car - with drastic results, I'm afraid! It took us the best part of the night to get a bag of sand into the tail of the car through a somewhat restricted aperture. Sand was used as our car was below the weight for its class.

85 By comparison, the Georges Boillot Cup Race was a monotonous occasion, unless you were fortunate enough to be able to see the score board. It was difficult to ascertain who held the lead on account of the intricate system under which the cars were handicapped. The race was won by Laly, driving a 3 litre Ariès. Campbell was second but was disqualified as he had exceeded the 10% allowed on the eliminating trial. This photo shows the 2 litre unblown Bugatti in touring form, passing the grandstand.

86 During September, the Surbiton MC organised a novel race on a fuel limitation basis over a distance of 150 miles. Each car was limited to a restricted amount of fuel, dependent on the car's cubic capacity. The cars had to be turned out in sports touring form, with wings, hood, windscreen, etc. Campbell had entered his 2 litre unblown Bugatti as used for the Georges Boillot Cup at Boulogne. His petrol allowance was 8½ gallons, compared with Dingle's Austin Seven's 4¾ gallons; by contrast, Barnato's Bentley was allowed 17¾ gallons. As usual, Campbell was unable to try the car until the day before the event, and I literally stood on my head, tuning the two horizontal Solex carburettors fitted, trying to get a reasonable performance from the limited amount of petrol allowed, when Campbell turned up to test the car. I was with him and unfortunately ran out of petrol near the Fork. I got a severe reprimand for wasting the old boy's time. So on the next test I was carrying a two-gallon tin of petrol on my lap. We were going pretty well when the ruddy engine caught fire. Campbell sensed this and yelled, 'The engine's on fire!'

By this time, things were getting pretty hot and I was about to eject the petrol can, which I had been nursing, overboard, when Campbell nudged me and yelled, 'Don't do that, you damned fool! There's 3 bob on that can!'

He switched off and we managed, with some help, to get back to the Paddock. Fortunately, the damage was not serious. He came in second after a very methodical drive. He was rather fed up when told he had 2 gallons left in the tank. Had he used more urge, he could have won. His average was 24 mpg at approximately 73 mph. This picture, taken after the race, shows the Skipper 'in a pensive mood'. the chap in the cap is the late Lionel Martin, designer of the Aston Martin car.

87 Campbell had entered a 1½ litre s/c Bugatti to compete in the British Grand Prix, due to take place on Saturday, 1st October. During some of our early practice laps, the car was running exceedingly well, until the Skipper decided to give it a short test the day preceding the combat. A sticking inlet valve was responsible for George, Paul Dutoit and 'your humble servant' working through and past the 2 o'clock session I mentioned at the beginning of this *Kaleidoscope*. With a set of new valves and guides fitted, we were replacing the cylinder blocks by 5 o'clock. Campbell, bright and breezy, arrived at 8.30 am and said, 'What was the trouble, lads?'

I mentioned how we had worked through the night. 'Oh, I *am* sorry, what infernal bad luck,' was his retort and he handed me a St Christopher badge to be fixed on the dashboard [wasn't I lucky!].

Campbell's opposing main forces were pretty strong: three works Delages to be driven by Benoist, Bourlier and Divo, and three works Bugattis in the hands of Materassi, Conelli and Chiron. At 12 noon, as you can see, the Skipper was on the Start Line, ready for the fray.

the Start Line at the beginning of the Railway Straight, he shot into the lead, much to everyone's surprise. Later he was overtaken by Materassi, who was driving at a furious pace and braking heavily when approaching the bends - quite a contrast to Bourlier, crouched in his low Delage, and appearing to make little effort. After ten laps, the order was: Divo [Delage], Bourlier [Delage], Benoist [Delage], with Chiron, Conelli and Campbell following in their Bugattis. At 30 laps, Conelli was in fourth place. On the 50th lap, Bourlier had taken the lead and Campbell was hanging on grimly in sixth place. At one stage, Campbell came into the pits to change tyres and take on fuel; he was followed in by Benoist, who had got away first. Later, an exhausted Conelli pushed his car from the Byfleet Banking into the pits, having run out of fuel. His car was taken over by Williams. Campbell retired on the 97th lap with valve trouble; the engine had been firing back down the induction pipe for quite a time which now resembled an exhaust pipe, on which I badly burned my right hand while looking for the cause. Benoist won the race, Bourlier was second, Divo third. The Bugatti driven by Chrion was the only Bugatti to finish and came in fourth.

left, Car No 6, at the start of that race. But if the troubles we had to run into had not been overcome, he might never had competed in that race ....

Realising that the works Bugattis used in the English Grand Prix were far superior to his own car, Campbell had approached Colonel Sorel, the director of Bugatti Ltd, who ran the distributing agency and servicing department for the patron at Molsheim. He had rented part of the old taxi garage at the lower end of Brixton Road, SE. As Conelli's car had not run the full distance of the Grand Prix and was still in good running order, Campbell wanted to purchase it and eventually made a deal with Colonel Sorel.

The car had been thoroughly checked over by the Bugatti team at Brixton and taken down to Brooklands for Campbell to test. After covering several laps, Campbell had returned to the Paddock, looking as pleased as a dog with two tails. The car at the time was running on Champion sparking plugs. Campbell's choice had always been KLG plugs. I asked him if he would be good enough to give the car another run using KLG. He stated he could see no point in doing this, but after much protesting, he agreed. A new set of KLGs were fitted, and he set out to do a further lap, but did not make it. We towed him back with one of the connecting rods sticking out of a hole in the crankcase.

---

88 Campbell was a past master at getting off the mark, and when Ebby's flag dropped on

89 Campbell's next ambition was to win the JCC 200-Mile Race. Here he is, third from

90 The Bugatti was using roller bearings for its big ends, and we did experience some trouble with broken con rods. No satisfactory explanation was given at that period and the plug incident I previously mentioned could have been coincidental. However, with just over a week to go, the car was transported back to Molsheim. The Hon Brian, or 'Bug' Lewis as we named him, was sent over to expedite the matter and drive the car back to England.

The car eventually arrived at 5 o'clock on Friday, 14th October, the day before the race. Campbell arrived at the Track pronto to test it and while braking hard through one of the chicanes, the front wheel brakes jammed and locked solid. The car was subsequently returned to our shed where George Miller, Percy Thomas and myself set about sorting things out. We were once again to see that ruddy clock on the wall creep up to 2 o'clock and keep going. We had soon sorted the brake problems out and done a fair amount of work on the engine when, about six o'clock, I removed the top of the gearbox to flush out and refill with oil. I could not believe my eyes: the second and third gears were practically non-existent on account of rough usage in gear changing. I hopefully rang Brixton, thinking in terms of a new gearbox, but could get no reply. The best I could do was to thoroughly clean the gearbox out and refill with fresh oil. I did not mention what I had found to the others, but quickly replaced the gearbox cover and its covering shield.

On reflection, as I went over to the bench,

George looked up and said,
'Hell, you look tired, Leo!'
Yes, I think I was.

---

91 On Saturday, 15th October, the 750cc, 1100cc and 1500cc classes were packed for the start of the JCC 200. Campbell was sitting in his car as tranquil as ever, and I had started the engine. Ebby had taken his position and I was all set to beat a hasty retreat before he raised his Starting Flag. At the very last moment, I leant over and yelled to the Skipper: 'Go easy when you change gear!'

He turned quickly and yelled, 'What? Why? Etc, etc!' But the flag fell and he was away, no doubt wondering whether it was possible for our car to run the distance without refuelling, barring other troubles, of course.

The race was to prove a three-way struggle between George Eyston, Morel driving an 1100cc Amilcar, and Campbell. Eyston held the lead for several laps, with Campbell in close pursuit, Morel bringing up the rear. All went well until the halfway stage when Campbell came into the pits, lamenting that his bloody gearbox had packed up. I sprang over the pit counter and asked what was wrong.

'I have no second and third gears, Villa,' he said.

'That's OK,' I replied. 'You have first and top,' and yelled over to George to help me get him rolling. He went off protesting - in not very polite terms. Each time he subsequently

passed the pits, he shook his fist in our direction.

However, he caught and passed Morel, in spite of his handicap. His average speed was 76.62 mph. The photo shows Malcolm, Mrs Campbell, Donald and Jean, with Hugh McConnell, the Scrutineer, sealing the engine for cc verification later.

92 At the close of the Brooklands season, George and I returned to Napiers. The engine and gearbox had now been installed. There had been some delay before the new crown wheels and pinion was delivered and our first task was to fit this now higher ratio. As the car had to be delivered to Barkers, the coachbuilders, for a very much modified body, designed I think by Pierson of Vickers, we really had to go all-out as we were already behind schedule.

Joan, my wife, bless her, suffered many an inconvenience, not knowing what time I would be home for a meal, to say nothing of the endless hours she spent alone when we were doing an all-night stint. We were now living in a new house at Tolworth, Surbiton, which I was hoping to purchase, and there was now an addition to the family: Joan bore me a son, whilst I was over in Boulogne - and he was named Leo, like his dad. Joan was always cheerful, loyal and encouraging. Indeed, I had a great deal to be thankful for. Incidentally, my wages at the time were five pounds per week, but we seemed to manage very well. This picture shows Joan with baby Leo, taken at Ascot.

DAYTONA AND BEYOND

Pressure was mounting on both sides of the Atlantic
to capture the coveted Land Speed Record.
Campbell's revised *Bluebird*, with bodywork by Arrol-Aster,
wrested it from Segrave, who replied with his all new Golden Arrow.
Meanwhile, the Skipper scoured Africa for a suitable expanse of flat sand
and was rewarded with three alarming aircraft experiences.
Despite all this, he found time to win races in France and Britain
in his new Grand Prix Delage
and to work his devoted team to the limit.

93 The Napier *Bluebird*, complete with its new, streamlined body, was returned to Napiers, and our task now was to fit the instrumentation and two new radiators for the engine coolant. Unlike its predecessor, the nose of the engine cowl was now completely sealed and two surface radiators fitted on the tail end of the car, adjacent to the road wheels. In the event of overheating, a detachable panel was fitted under the nose of the engine cowl. To decrease the air resistance fairings were fitted behind the road wheels. A shallow tail fin for directional stability was added with a detachable section to increase its height, should this be found necessary. The sides of the cockpit had been increased to

offer the Skipper more protection. Lord Wakefield of Hythe was extremely interested, and visited Napiers with Campbell to see our latest creation. He later arranged that the holder of the record should be presented with a trophy to be known as the Wakefield Trophy and a cheque for £1000.

---

94 Campbell's bid to take Segrave's record created considerable interest. It was rumoured that Campbell had challenged Segrave to a race, if he was prepared to bring the 1000hp *Slug* along to Daytona. Knowing Campbell, I feel sure that this was just a

publicity stunt with no foundation whatsoever. Unlike the 450 Napier, the new engine could not possibly be started by hand and we had some difficulty in getting a device known as a gas starter to do this work. Briefly, the gas starter is a unit carrying a small two stroke engine, driving an air compressor, delivering a pressure of 80 psi. The high pressure is conducted through a pipe attached to a main air distributor on the Napier engine, from which separate, small-bore pipes feed compressed air into the cylinders.

The picture shows George and myself completing details before the car's despatch to the packers, LEP Transport at Chiswick.

95   A preview was arranged at Napiers for the Press and the industrial firms who had subscribed either in kind or in cash to make the project possible.

Subsequently, the car was despatched to LEP Transport, where a huge packing case had been constructed for its shipment to the USA. During a conversation I had with the Skipper, he mentioned that two American cars would be there to challenge him: a young, well-known track driver, Frank Lockhart with his Stutz Black Hawk Special, a small car with an engine developing 400hp and, by contrast, the Triplex, an enormous juggernaut of a car, equipped with three Liberty aero engines. This car was designed by a wealthy business-man, a Mr White, and was to be driven by another well-known American ace, called Ray Keech. Although it all sounded very exciting, it certainly gave us something to ponder about.

This picture was taken at LEP Transport of the car being packed. The small Bugatti model was taken over as a showpiece.

---

96   Campbell and his wife, with the *Bluebird* team, comprising five bods - Joe Coe from Napiers and his partner, Walter ['Fiddle'] Hicks, Steve MacDonald of Dunlops, George Miller and myself - embarked on the *SS Berengaria* at Southampton early February 1928. I think the *Berengaria* was formerly the expatriated German liner *Vaterland*. The car in its enormous packing case was lashed down on the top deck.

Campbell at that time did own a 30ft motor cruiser called *Bill Duan*, but owing to spells of sickness when cruising with him, I'm afraid I did not take readily to sea travel. Mrs

Campbell, nevertheless, consoled me by pointing out that a vessel of the *Berengaria*'s size neither rocked nor rolled. Our cabin was on the small size, situated in the tourist quarters, and after airing our grievances with Campbell, a larger and better cabin was allocated for us. On the second day out, we ran into some foul weather and I'm afraid I lost all interest in the journey, in America, in fact in the whole shooting match, until we arrived in smoother waters, nearing New York. Apparently, the storm was so severe that half the crew went sick and the damage done to crockery, etc, escalated into some hundreds of pounds.

---

97   The following morning after our dis-embarkation at New York, we had to present

ourselves at the dock, as the car and our numerous cases of spare parts, including one spare engine, had to be checked by the Customs officers. That same evening, the team boarded the *Dixie Flyer* at Pennsylvania Station for Daytona. As there would be some delay before the car, travelling by freight car to Daytona, was expected, the Skipper and Mrs Campbell stayed on in New York for press conferences, etc. We arrived at Daytona late the following evening, after a very relaxing journey, although the Maryland ham served en route did not exceed the quality served at the Beach Hotel. On arrival at Daytona, we were welcomed by a handful of the city's dignitaries, and shown to our quarters. They were most disappointing: a series of cubicles situated over the garage that was to house *Bluebird*, infested by mosquitoes and other unusual midges. The following morning we raised hell and were smartly

directed to more habitable quarters.

With time on our hands, we were introduced to Frank Lockhart, one of our opponents, who took us along to see his car. It was indeed a super looking job. It weighed less than 3000 lbs and was powered by two eight-cylinder Miller engines, coupled together and supercharged.

---

98 Owing to adverse winds which would leave the surface of the beach in anything but a suitable condition, the delays were considerable. Our first trial run ended in near disaster. Campbell took the car on a southward run. Going very fast, he struck a very uneven patch of sand and the car became airborne. He hit the sand with an almighty

crash and went into a broadside skid. Fortunately, he managed to correct this, but on inspection much damage to the car was the result. The undershield was torn off and was found some distance away, rolled up like a map. The shock absorber mountings had broken off and the structure supporting the pilot's seat damaged. With some effort, Campbell managed to get out of the cockpit, but was limping badly, having for the second time received a blow on the base of his spine.

Mustering outside help to machine us a complete set of shock absorber mountings in steel, it took more or less three days and nights before we were able to run again. We did have several other setbacks. But on 19th February, although the conditions were far from ideal and despite an almighty skid on a loose patch of sand, the Skipper raised the record to 206.956 mph, taking Segrave's record.

Lockhart
↓

STUTZ BLACK HAWK
SPECIAL
MADE IN INDIANAPOLIS

WRECK OF LOCKHARTS BLACK HAWK
Daytona Beach, Fla

99 Frank Lockhart made a timed trial run on the Stutz Black Hawk that same day, but only succeeded in clocking 181 mph. He then decided that the conditions were not up to his expectation and all being well he would make the attempt on the following day.

Campbell told us that *Bluebird*'s potential had not been reached and he would like to make another timed run. The Triplex Special was not given permission to attempt a record run, as it had not been fitted with reverse gear, nor clutch. Ray Keech did, however, make a trial run and was badly scalded when the main water-circulating pipe between the

rear and front engine came adrift.

The following day, *Bluebird* was on the beach with the team standing by, ready to run again should Lockhart eclipse Campbell's record. A slight breeze was blowing down the course at the time and Lockhart decided to make his first run from south to north - unlike Campbell's north to south. The announcer stated that he had started his run and soon after we heard the drone of his engine, before it appeared to cut out. We later learnt that Lockhart had entered the Measured Mile and was going very fast when his car veered seawards and, hitting the surf, became

airborne, turning a complete somersault and landing the right side up, facing the shore. It was practically submerged and Lockhart was trapped in the cockpit. But the spectators made a superhuman effort and managed to drag the car out of the water where the side of the cockpit was cut away to release Lockhart. The car was a write-off, but fortunately Lockhart suffered no serious injury.

———————————————

100 This is a rear view of the Triplex Special, which was to be driven by Ray Keech,

but was scratched on account of its construction not meeting with the scrutineer's approval. But the Triplex did appear at Daytona later that year and beat Campbell's record with a speed of 207.55, as opposed to Campbell's average of 206.95. Campbell lamented the fact that he had been persuaded not to have made a second run while he was out at Daytona, on account of Frank Lockhart's mishap, especially as we were later to find that *Bluebird*'s potential was well beyond the speed the car had then attained. This situation was to develop into a tussle between Segrave and Campbell during a memorable 1929 so as to regain the coveted LSR Laurel Crown for England.

---

101 We returned home from the USA on the *Berengaria*. Fortunately, we enjoyed a smoother passage than on the voyage out. On arrival at the dockside, Campbell was welcomed by the Mayoress of Southampton and the Skipper was to enjoy many functions laid on in his honour.

Bluebird was duly unpacked at LEP Transport and taken to Brooklands Track, where it was put on display in our workshop, the donations received being sent to the Weybridge Cottage Hospital. Later, Campbell made some fast demonstration runs round the Mountain Circuit.

The picture shows *Bluebird* at Brooklands with Campbell in the cockpit, ready to start the engine. Note the small unit on the stand by the front wheel; this was the gas start that supplied the compressed air for starting the Napier engine. The term 'gas starter' refers to the air drawn into the compressor passing through a carburettor, thus supplying an atomised mixture of petrol to the engine.

102 It was during 1928 that I was to accompany Campbell when he visited the Delage factory to purchase two of their very successful and famous Delage 1½ litre s/c Grand Prix cars. Possibly my command of the French lingo promoted this. Although we did not have the opportunity of meeting 'Old Man' Delage himself, we were cordially conducted through the works and had the choice of three cars that were then available. Apart from the cars, quite a number of spare parts, refuelling and pit equipment was placed at our disposal. I cannot recall the name of the hotel we stayed at in Paris, but do remember having dinner with the Skipper and devouring an enormous plate of delicious asparagus.

The two cars with their spares, etc, arrived in England; this picture shows one of them being towed past the Brooklands clubhouse and over to our workshop in mid-June. We experienced some trouble during tests; apparently the factory had changed the carburettors and were now using a slightly longer air intake. Campbell stated the car had fantastic acceleration up to 5000 rpm, after which the speed would fall off. We checked everything but could locate nothing amiss. By luck, he made one run with the engine cover removed and for the first time he was able to reach maximum rpm. On investigation we found out that, at speed, the engine cover deflected a partially restricted airflow from going into the intake.

103 The 1½ litre s/c Delage was indeed a masterpiece and will always remain my favourite for performance and reliability. It outclassed all other marques at that period. With a bore x stroke of 55.8mm x 76mm, the engine developed 170hp using 6.5:1 compression ratio and boost pressure of 7.5 psi. Two valves per cylinder were used, actuated by two overhead çamshafts. Maximum permissible rpm were 8400. The car had five speeds and 4-wheel servo-assisted brakes. Lubrication was based on the dry sump principle.

Campbell told me the Delage was in a class of its own, and entered it for the Junior Car Club 200-Mile Race on 21st July. Apart from a thorough check-up, there was little to do to the car and Campbell's win was a foregone conclusion, following the same course as in 1927.

The Delage, No 3, ran the race with monotonous regularity. He made one pit stop on the 37th lap for a tyre and fuel check, and was off again until the end of the race. He covered the distance in 2 hrs 34 mins with an average speed of 78.34 mph, his nearest rival crossing the Finishing Line 12 mins 12 secs later.

104 With the smile of victory on his face, Campbell is wheeled into the Paddock after his very successful victory. Also in the picture is your humble servant in white overalls, who had very good reasons for enjoying the occasion, too. Hugh McConnell, the well-known and popular scrutineer during those happy days, was also present with his coil of wire and seal, which he used to prevent the engine cover being opened until the cubic capacity of the engine had been calibrated by Ebby and his assistant scrutineer.

After a relaxed Sunday at home with my family, I returned to Brooklands to remove the cylinders, etc, for this check to be carried out - the engine being re-assembled when all was found to be in order. I did not realise it then, but the removal of that cylinder block was to cause us some considerable concern when the car appeared in its next race at Boulogne.

105 The Ulster International Tourist Trophy Race at Belfast was to be our next sortie, and for this Campbell had entered a 2.3 s/c Bugatti 4 seater tourer. We had previously experienced some trouble with the petrol tank on a similar car and, to overcome this, a tank with a double skin containing a sealing compound had been specially constructed. Viscount Curzon [Lord Howe] had entered a similar Bugatti.

The race was unusual in many respects. The engines were switched off after warming-up and the drivers and mechanics lined up on the opposite side of the road. When Ebby's flag fell, they raced to their cars, raised the hoods, then started their engines and were away! On the completion of two laps, the cars were stopped at their pits and the hoods were lowered to complete the 30 laps, totalling 410 miles. We got away well.

Birkin in a Bentley, hotly pursued by Howe, covered the first lap. I think we were lying fifth. On the second lap, I noticed the air pressure in the fuel tank falling, and had to keep using the hand-pump to maintain 2 psi. Nearing the pit on the second lap, Campbell shouted something about, 'The hood! Don't lose any time!'

We screeched to a halt and I left the car in double-quick time, hotly followed by Campbell - and was horrified to notice the rear of the car well and truly in flames.

106 In no time at all, the car was an inferno; clouds of dense black smoke were drifting across the track, almost obscuring the cars that were racing through them. Frantic efforts were made to remove the gallons of fuel laid out on our pit counter for refuelling. While many fire extinguishing methods were brought into use in an effort to douse the flames. Campbell and I resorted to hand extinguishers, but these were useless. The heat was intense and then the fuel tank exploded and spewed flaming spirit on the ground under the car. Until the last vestige of flaming spirit had burned itself out, we could only stand by, looking helplessly on, until the car was completely burnt out.

Lord Howe was forced to retire when he had covered half the distance, owing to his fuel tank disintegrating. He was, however, more fortunate as the leaking fuel did not ignite. Campbell was heard to remark,

'Well, that's the luck of this game. That car cost me £1500 and it was not insured'.

The race was won by Kaye Don driving a Lea Francis, followed by Leon Cushman driving an Alvis.

---

107 Campbell's next engagement was to be at Boulogne, where he had entered the Delage for the Trophée National Race. Owing to our misadventures at Belfast, there were some delays, resulting in a tight schedule so as to be present for the race on 9th September.

Apart from replacing the cylinder block on the Delage after the 200-Mile Race, very little had been done to the car and there were one or two items that I was rather doubtful about. With little time to spare, we duly arrived in Boulogne and on tests ran into a severe bout of oiling-up plugs. Removing the cylinders had displaced the steel piston rings and we had left without spares. Delage in Paris were consulted and a mechanic was despatched with new piston rings, etc. By the time he arrived, George and I had removed the cylinders and had fitted new brake shoes. We worked all through the night and by early morning the engine was running and ready for test. We were still in trouble, however, as the engine would tend to oil up its plugs if allowed to idle too long. Running in the new rings was the only solution. So with the hose pipe circulating cold water through the radiator, the engine was kept running as often as possible at 3000 rpm. After warming up a new set of spark plugs were fitted and Campbell drove up to the Starting Line on the 9th with only seconds to go before the flag fell. We started the engine, and with the exhaust roaring, he got away to a typically prompt start.

Here is Campbell on his first lap, leaving a trail of smoke as he passes through a cobble-stoned French village.

---

108 As Campbell streaked away in the lead, your humble servant, George and the French

mechanic hastily returned to our pit to put things in order. The article that took precedence over all else was the number of KLG plugs, all removed from their boxes ready to hand with a set of 'softs' we intended to risk using, should the worst happen.

Campbell's progress was announced, passing through La Capelle, Le Wast, Alincthun and Desures - well in the lead. As he flashed by us on the first lap, a cloud of smoke still trailed from the exhaust. His nearest opponent was Gauthier driving a 2 litre s/c Bugatti. The situation became tense when, on the third lap, it was reported that Campbell had stopped at Fort Mahon. Gauthier came in, but left in a hurry when his excitable pit manager shouted, 'Avant! Campbell has packed up!'

Some moments later, to our intense joy, the Delage passed the pits, going very fast indeed on its final lap. His winning speed was 72.078 mph and he covered the distance in 3 hours 50 mins 34 secs, winning the Trophée National for the second year in succession.

We later learnt how a detached earth wire on the ignition switch had caused Campbell's stoppage at Port Mahon and how, after speedily diagnosing this, he had ripped the ignition wire from the magneto and pressed on. The picture shows the Skipper on his final lap, with a now very much diminished smoke trail.

109 In spite of Campbell's many other activities, his one great ambition was to regain the LSR for his country, and the Napier *Bluebird* had been transported to Arrol Asters, the well-known manufacturer at Dumfries in Scotland, where a new super-streamlined body had been designed and was now under construction.

Segrave, equally as ambitious as Campbell, had found a wealthy distiller to back his project and Major Irving had designed him a record-breaking car to be called *The Golden Arrow*, which was now under construction at the KLG works in Kingston Vale.

I was more than pleasantly surprised when Giulio Foresti, my old boss, paid Campbell a visit one day at Brooklands. He was looking older and had lost some of his hair, otherwise none the worse after his serious accident and miraculous escape when his car *Djelmo* overturned spectacularly at Pendine in 1927 during an attempt to beat Segrave's record of 203 mph [see above].

He did not seem keen to talk about his misadventure other than explaining, 'Djelmo! Villa, she go very fast, but I not possible to hold!' He had now returned to circuit racing on the Continent, having decided that record-breaking was not his métier.

110 Here is *The Golden Arrow* under construction at the Robinhood Engineering Works [KLG]. Studying the chassis is Harold Irving, a relative of her designer, Major Irving. Segrave had made it publicly known that he intended making his LSR with *The Golden Arrow* at Daytona. Campbell, however, had different ideas.

Apart from the tide and narrowness of the beach at Daytona, he was not keen on being pressurised by other opposition, as he had been during his LSR attempt at Daytona earlier in the year. Although Ray Keech, the driver of the Triplex, had been killed during a circuit race in the States, White, the owner of Triplex, intended nominating another driver to pilot his car and increase its present performance, thus keeping the LSR in America. Following Campbell's public search of a suitable stretch of terrain in this country, other than Pendine, information came to hand that a long stretch of hard sand did exist somewhere in the Sahara Desert. His adventurous spirit reacted favourably to an expedition and he had soon purchased a light Moth aeroplane. With Flight Lieutenant Don [at that time pilot to the Prince of Wales], they set off from Hendon Aerodrome early one Saturday morning for an unknown destination in the middle of the Sahara.

111 To make sure that our time would be fully occupied during his absence, true to form, Campbell had prepared a list of work that would keep George Miller and myself fully occupied for an indefinite period. He had acquired a secondhand Morris Oxford for my use, in particular to transport me to Arrol Asters in Scotland, with specific orders to collect a circular radiator from Messrs Serck, the manufacturers in Birmingham, designed to conform with *Bluebird*'s new, streamlined body. George Miller was despatched to our workshop at Brooklands to modify some gas starters Campbell had purchased and packed such tools and spares as would be needed for our new attempt on the LSR.

When I arrived at Arrol Asters with the new radiator stowed in the boot of the Morris, I was conducted to a very large building, where I found that the work on the new body was in a very advanced stage. A higher rear axle ratio was being made for the car, which I was to fit should it be completed in time. I was working in unusual surroundings as the major part of the building was used for the mass production of hand-built bodies for the Arrol Aster cars. Mass-production at that time was in its infancy. A set of narrow gauge rails ran the entire length of the shop. Running on these rails was a series of wheeled, low-platform vehicles on which were mounted car bodies in various stages of construction. A bell would be rung at timed intervals and the assembly line would roll; as the line stopped at each section, a different crew would descend on it to fit doors, windscreens, etc, before the line re-started on its way.

Looking back, it was amusing to see the work force in action when the situation 'got out of control', which it often did!

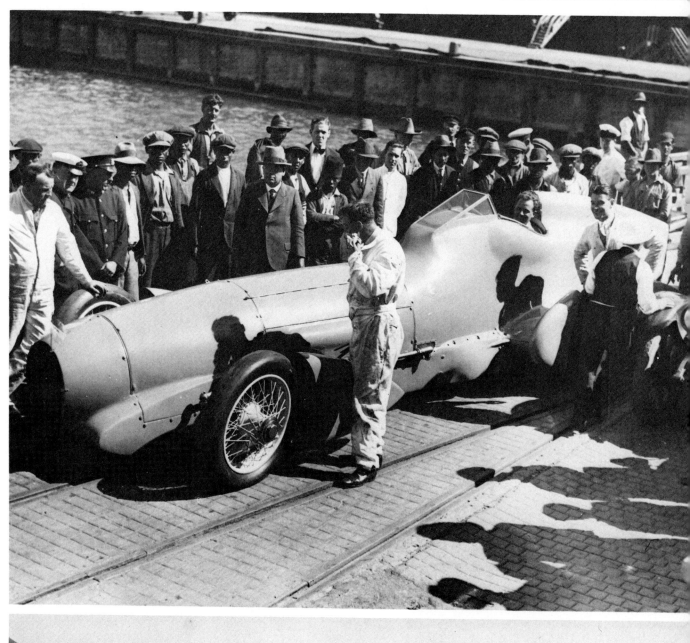

112 Campbell's search for a new track in the Sahara nearly ended in disaster. After a fruitless search over hundreds of miles of desert, they were homeward bound when the Moth suffered engine failure crossing the Atlas Mountains. A forced landing on a rock-strewn beach threw them on the mercy of a crowd of Riffian bandits, who stole all their meagre belongings, including their camera and the vital negatives they had taken. A Spanish naval vessel rescued the plane and Campbell and Don, his pilot, returned home by sea.

Campbell's experiences, however, created worldwide interest and, within a few days of his return, he received a cable from South Africa, stating that there was a site north-east of Cape Town that would be ideal for an LSR. Not wishing to miss an opportunity, Campbell appointed a friend, Mr Walters, to go out and survey the site. Later receiving a favourable report, he decided to try his luck and a passage was booked on the SS Caernarvon Castle for himself and family, the team, Bluebird, and several cases of tyres and equipment. Our final destination was to be a dried-up lake 450 miles from Cape Town, known as Verneuk Pan, an Afrikaans word meaning 'To cheat or mislead'. We embarked at Southampton early January, arriving in Cape Town on 1st February, some three weeks later. This picture shows Bluebird removed from its case after unloading at Cape Town.

113 The translation [Verneuk - to cheat or mislead] was no understatement. This, to date, was to be the toughest assignment we were to tackle. Our temporary working quarters were with the Thornycroft Co in Cape Town, where Bluebird had been transported. The Austin Co put a car at Campbell's disposal and the Skipper lost no time in making his first visit to the Pan. When he returned to Cape Town some days later, he called the team together and told us he was not at all happy about the Pan and the way the situation had been handled: leaving Cape Town, the road was reasonably good for about 80 miles, but then you crossed the Karoo Desert where roads did not then exist [see above], and to use his expression, 'Bloody tracks lead in all directions, you could get lost. I'm afraid we're in for a rough time, lads'.

To make matters worse, the whole surface of the Pan was covered with stones and small pieces of shale embedded in the dried mud. Unless these could be cleared away, the tyres would be cut to shreds. Additionally, Walters, his representative, had been ill-advised and the 7 miles of track that had been partially cleared ran east-west - directly into the sun. The situation looked hopeless until Campbell was introduced to a very capable man called Mr Nesbitt, the Road Engineer for the North-West Cape; Nesbitt's chief, Mr Beck, realised Campbell's predicament and sanctioned Nesbitt to take control of the situation.

114 Nesbitt realised the significance of removing the sharp pieces of shale projecting through the mud as his foremost task, and decided to clear a 50ft strip down the centre of the 120ft width that Campbell needed. To do the work, he needed more labour, a roller and water. His plan was to remove the stones and shale by sweeping and scraping away the surface, then relaying the track with a mixture of the original pan clay and water.

Nesbitt's appeal for the necessary equipment was met with enthusiasm, and a grader and tractor, plus lorries, and several sums of money, were donated to the project by the sporting population of South Africa. Labour did present problems as the kaffirs, who would have jumped at the chance of earning a few shillings a day, were scarce in this part of the country, whilst the 'Cape Coloured' boys from Cape Town suffered sickness and many were to desert. Four hundred hands were anticipated, but only one hundred stayed till the job was completed. Another problem was a supply of water. This had to be transported from Muller's Farm, five miles away. The Town Council of Germiston loaned us a roller which was driven up over 120 miles by one of their engineers. Tents of all descriptions were also made available for our needs.

The picture shows a gang of 'the boys' re-surfacing the track after the stones and shale had been removed.

115 The team, consisting of Steve Mac-donald from Dunlops, Joe Coe from Napiers, George Miller and I were working on *Bluebird* in Cape Town, enjoying the comfort of a first-class hotel at Cape Point and fortunately missing all the heat, flies and the many inconveniences that Verneuk was noted for. The new ratio for the rear axle was one of our main tasks as this had not been completed in time for me to fit while at Arrol Asters [see caption 111].

Campbell's Moth aeroplane that he had used for his Sahara expedition had been repaired and shipped to Cape Town and now he was using this as transport to and from the Pan, to save time and avoid the miserable journey over that Karoo Desert. Campbell had the occasional meeting with us to report progress, but frequent delays at Verneuk through one cause or another did give the Skipper some concern as he was more than anxious to beat the American record before Segrave, who at the time was at Daytona, also delayed by unfavourable weather.

It was now early March and owing to a crack in the propeller of his plane, Campbell decided on other transportation, accepting a lift in the plane of a wealthy African sports-man. The events that took place on that flight to the track gave us all good reason to think that Verneuk might well be jinxed.

116 Their flight *to* the Pan was uneventful and on the return journey they alighted at a small dorp called Calvinia. After a short stay, they were taking off again when the pilot found himself in difficulties and ran into a tree. Campbell suffered severe injury to his nose, having been pitched forward onto some of the plane's bracing wires on impact with the ground; his nose was to be scarred for life. He also suffered some concussion due to the reserve petrol tank breaking adrift and falling on his head. The pilot had his skull fractured in two places and the machine was a total write-off - as you can see. A plane was despatched from Cape Town to bring Campbell back and while taxiing across the airfield on arrival, a violent gust of wind caught the machine and turned it over, pitching Campbell out, causing him still further injuries! He received proper medical attention and was confined to his bedroom for three weeks. On the second day of his enforced retirement, he received news that torrential rains had fallen on Verneuk and all the work of the past months had been washed out. It was ironic then to be told that not a drop of rain had fallen on Verneuk Pan for the past seven years.

117 Campbell was well on the road to recovery and on the evening of his forty-fifth birthday, while having dinner with his wife and some friends, he received a message from Reuters, stating that Segrave had broken the existing LSR with an average speed of 231.36 mph. The photo shows *The Golden Arrow* triumphant at Daytona.

Campbell realised that his chances of surpassing that speed looked remote. The fact that the Pan, with its rarified atmosphere was 3000ft above sea level, probably accounting for an 11% loss of power, would in all likelihood cancel out the advantage we anticipated on account of *Bluebird*'s new streamlined body and lessened air resistance. Campbell realised he could better Ray Keech's record of 207.5 mph by a substantial margin, but 231 mph was a different matter.

However, win or lose, he decided to have a go and preparations were made for our transportation with the car to Verneuk. This was to create more problems as the special six-wheeled truck allocated to Campbell had been sold. A frantic search was made to find a vehicle large enough to carry *Bluebird* in her packing case. Eventually, a much shorter FWD truck was located. To overcome our difficulties, *Bluebird*, in its case, was loaded onto the one railway truck and the FWD truck on another, and consigned to the railhead at Zak River, 80 miles from the Pan.

8665.

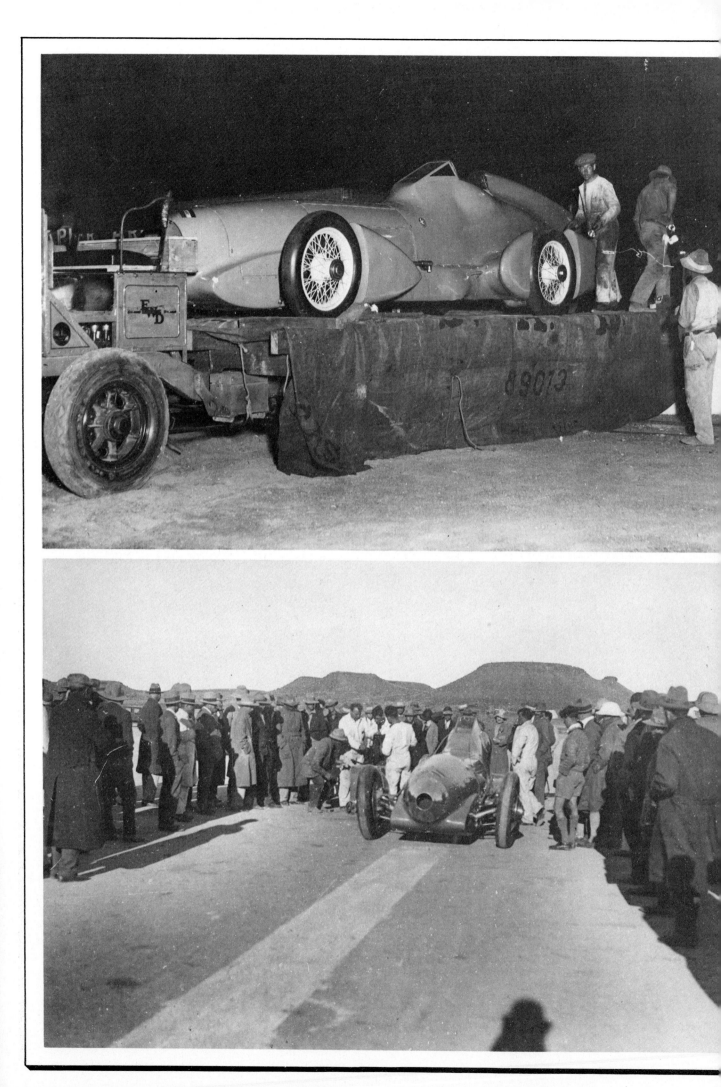

118 George Miller and myself travelled up by rail with the car and equipment and arrived at the railhead of Zak River during the early hours, after a 48-hour journey. Removing the car from its case and loading it onto the lorry proved no easy task, as there was but little illumination and we had to resort to hand torches. To make our task more difficult, we were told to keep the car covered with a tarpaulin, as a Cape Town newspaper had been given the exclusive rights to cover Campbell's activities. As the picture shows, we were not entirely successful, and some cunning blighter did get into the act with his flash-gun. *Bluebird*'s packing case was left at the railhead.

Our journey to the Pan was quite a nightmare on account of the state of such roads that existed being partly washed away due to the recent rainstorm. In places, we had to cross several fords of unknown depth that were carrying the water away from the hills and higher ground through which we were travelling. But, by the grace of God, we arrived at the Pan, dog-tired and hungry.

---

119 A large pit had been dug by the *kaffirs* into which the FWD lorry was backed and, after unloading, *Bluebird* was pushed into a

large marquee which, apart from being our workshop, was also to be the team's sleeping quarters. While in Cape Town, we made our own beds of wood and canvas, having been forewarned that the possibility of being stung by infectious insects was less likely if you slept a little distance from the mud floor.

To me, Verneuk looked foreboding and unfriendly - just miles and miles of 'Sweet Fanny Adams' - flat, dried mud as far as the eye could see. During the day, the heat was intense and infested with flies. There was a shortage of water and washing facilities amounted to nil. The Skipper had a small tent pitched alongside our marquee, and rough and ready as it was, we were behind him and keen to get on with the job. A white line, 12 miles long and 18 inches wide, had been painted down the centre of the course for his guidance and he made several trial runs. But 225 mph appeared to be the car's maximum and Campbell realised that he did not stand an earthly of exceeding Segrave's 231.

---

120 To add to our worries, we suffered a severe dust storm, which blew down many of the tents, including Campbell's. Had it not been for the superhuman efforts of many willing helpers hanging onto the guide ropes

of *Bluebird*'s marquee, this would have, without doubt, been blown down too. Following the storm, much time was spent removing the dust from our equipment, tools, etc.

Campbell had now decided that to prove his car's capabilities, he intended to go after the 5-Mile and 5-Kilo records. His intentions were dicey on account of parts of the track being broken up during some of his previous trials and runs. This, in turn, had damaged his tyres, and frequent changes had now left him with a limited number of spares. Steve MacDonald, Dunlop's representative, had his work cut out coping with the situation; so George and I pitched in to help him remove some of the outer covers - no easy task. Our other problem was having to make our runs at dawn, before sun-up, otherwise Campbell's vision would be hopelessly impaired by running into the sun's early morning glare.

On Thursday, 25th April, *Bluebird* was pushed to the starting point. After inspecting the track, the Skipper took his place in the pilot's seat and said, 'OK, chaps. Start her up!'

With the gas starter running, there followed an almighty roar from *Bluebird*'s engine and when the pipe and starting cable had been removed, he waved his arm and was away.

121 Although provision had been made for the Skipper to stop and change his tyres after the first run, he did not do this. Instead, turning in a wide circle, he made his return run. Looking unperturbed and with a broad grin, he coasted towards us and exclaimed, 'Well, chaps, I gave her the lot, and think I've done it! You know, I hit 229 mph on my return run but could squeeze no more .

His attempts on the 5-Mile and 5-Kilo records at least gave us all some satisfaction. The 5-Kilo Record now stood to Campbell's credit at 216.5 mph, well over Segrave's best at 202.6 mph. The 5-Mile Record, formerly held by the French at 146 mph, he raised to 212.8 mph. His rear tyres were devoid of their rubber casing and he had made the return run on the bare canvas. The photo shows *Bluebird* being pushed back to base after its final run.

Campbell left for Cape Town the following day, leaving us to pack up and return to the Zak River railhead to pack *Bluebird* in its case and load it onto a six-wheeled, brand new Thornycroft lorry that had been despatched from England. The cases of tyres, tools, etc, were loaded onto the FWD lorry and we then left the railhead at Zak River for Cape Town.

122 I think we all left Verneuk Pan with a sense of relief. So much effort was put into that venture and so much had gone wrong.

There was more in the Afrikaans' underlying meaning to the word *Verneuk* than we had given them credit for, and we were all under the impression that our bad luck would remain behind us on that infernal dried-up lake. But strangely, this was not to be. On our return journey, the driver of the FWD lorry ran off the road and finished upside down in a ravine. Fortunately, he escaped without injury. Campbell was in a collision with another car before he left Cape Town and the Castrol representative who was with us at Verneuk had a bad skid at Cape Town and the hired car he was driving was a total write-off.

Campbell returned to England and left George and myself to be in attendance with the car, which was displayed in Cape Town, Johannesburg, Pretoria, Kimberley and Durban. We were on tour for nearly two months and later returned home in the *SS Balmoral Castle*. The Napier-Arrol-Aster *Bluebird* was never run again, but became a showpiece. Its last public appearance was in the Lord Mayor's Show in 1929. It was towed in the procession by a 4½ litre Bentley. That was quite a day out, but I did not have the privilege of going to the Lord Mayor's luncheon, which Campbell had told me would be my bonus.

Finally, the car occupied a corner of our workshop at Brooklands, gathering dust,

frequently subject to Campbell's abusive remarks about 'the money that bloody car cost me!'

The picture shows your humble servant being towed through the City of London to join the Lord Mayor's procession.

123 I was not aware of the facts until I returned to this country, but a tragedy did occur following Henry Segrave's magnificent record with *The Golden Arrow* at Daytona:

The Triplex car, powered by three 400hp Liberty aero-engines, which previously held the LSR at 207.55 mph in 1928, had been modified and her wealthy owner, White, had decided that, with the power available, he could better Segrave's record. His mechanic, Lee Bible who, I think, had carried out the modifications, was appointed to drive the monster. Apparently Lee Bible lost control of the car when travelling at over 200 mph and was killed. A photographer, using a hand-wound movie camera, was taking a shot of the car racing towards him. Sensing danger, he attempted to make a hasty retreat, but only ran into the path of the oncoming car, to be killed instantly. Incredible as it may seem, his camera was found where he had left it, still standing and undamaged.

TOWARDS THE MAGICAL 300

As, one by one, his compatriots were killed in their quest for the LSR,
Sir Malcolm, as he became, showed great courage
in striving for the elusive 300 mph barrier.
In 'lighter moments' he drove his new GP Mercedes with tremendous flair
and then, largely on patriotic grounds, he switched to the famous
Sunbeam Tiger and Tigress to back 'the old country'.
Leo Villa watched the mounting pressures and gradually grew to understand
the Skipper's complex character that made him difficult to work for
but yet provoked deep loyalty amongst all who were close to him.

124 Segrave was knighted for his grand efforts at Daytona and later retired from car racing to concentrate on recapturing the World Water Speed Record from Gar Wood, the American speedboat champion. Lord Wakefield financed the construction of a new speedboat, *Miss England II*, powered by two Rolls-Royce s/c aero engines. On 13th June 1930, in an endeavour to exceed a speed of 100 mph on Lake Windermere, Campbell's old rival lost his life when the hydroplane went out of control; one of the riding mechanics also died.

At the time, the Skipper had set his sights on 300 mph and designs to achieve this were well advanced. He was more than distressed when he heard the news of Segrave's tragedy, but this in no way deterred him from going ahead with his plans.

He had now purchased a 7100cc supercharged Mercedes, which he intended to enter for the Irish International Grand Prix. To get the feel of the car, he ran it in the Mountain Speed Handicap at Brooklands. The circuit started along the old Finishing Straight, swept up to the Banking under the Members' Bridge to Chronograph Corner, and back into the Finishing Straight. Ten laps had to be covered. It was a handicap race and although Campbell was not spectacular on the corners, he took the lead on the seventh lap and came in first.

125 Campbell, driving his s/c Mercedes, left Povey Cross early in July bound for Dublin, where he had entered his car for the Irish Grand Prix. Mrs Campbell, myself and a young enthusiast who had now replaced George Miller were the Skipper's passengers. We arrived at Liverpool during the afternoon and boarded the *SS Lady Leinster*, docking at the North Wall, Dublin.

The other two Mercedes made up the team - one owned and driven by Lord Howe, the third, a works car to be driven by Herr Caracciola, the German ace. The photo, left to right, shows Earl Howe, the Skipper and Caracciola. Campbell and Howe were using the same garage, but Caracciola preferred his own private lock-up. During the practice laps, Campbell broke the lap record on two occasions and was warmly congratulated by Caracciola and his wife. 'How do you do it?' was repeatedly phrased by the Germans.

We had little trouble, although at the time I think both Howe and Campbell, as well as myself, were lulled into a false sense of security by the compliments paid both from the Press and our German buddies. Opposing

the Mercedes was the 4½ litre Bentley team, to be driven by Birkin, Chassagne and Harcourt-Wood. The great Le Mans Race had taken place during the previous month, when Caracciola was defeated by the Bentley team. No doubt the German ace had every intention of now reversing the situation.

---

126 The previous day's race for 1500cc, 1100cc and 750cc was won by Victor Gillow, driving his 1100cc Riley in 3 hrs 36 mins with an average speed of 72.20 mph. Much speculation was raised on the following day's race and Tim Birkin, driving the 4½ litre Bentley, was the popular favourite, possibly because he was driving a British car and patriotism came into the picture very strongly. Both Campbell and Howe were criticised for driving German cars. The progress of the race was not easy to follow on account of the handicap, in favour of the Bentleys' 4500cc as opposed to the Mercedes' 7020cc - the Bentleys receiving two laps in their favour.

On the morning of Saturday, 19th July 1930, the Starting Flag, lowered by President

Cosgrave, was followed by the ear-splitting noise of exhausts, as the starter motors of the 19 contestants whirred their engines into action. As you can see, Caracciola took the lead instantly in Car No 3, followed by Campbell, Car No 1, and Lord Howe, Car No 2, hotly pursued by Tim Birkin in his Bentley. Then it started to rain. As Caracciola was known to be a past master driving on wet roads, the now prevailing conditions no doubt gave him some satisfaction.

---

127 The rain most certainly slowed many of the cars up, but Caracciola ploughed firmly on. He had a very bad skid when his car gyrated down the road for five circles; fortunately for him, the road was clear at the time.

When approaching the corner at Gough Statue, Caracciola skidded onto the grass verge, Birkin in the Bentley close behind slid sideways alongside him. During the afternoon, Birkin and Campbell [Alfa Romeo] were leading on handicap. Campbell was

losing ground due to his clutch slipping. He stopped at the pits to refuel and I injected the contents of a Pyrene fire extinguisher into the clutch housing; this did cure the trouble, but some laps later he was in trouble again. Later that afternoon, Birkin drew into the pits with his engine on fire. He was quickly underway again but the stop cost him nearly three minutes - almost one lap. On the 40th lap, the order was: Birkin 1st, Caracciola 2nd, Campbell 3rd, Earl Howe 4th. Then Birkin suffered two pit stops and Caracciola took the lead. From there on, the ace dominated the race, to the extent that he was able to reduce his speed and romp home an easy winner. Campari's Alfa came 2nd, Lord Howe 3rd - Campbell unplaced.

The sequel to Caracciola's success at Dublin was brought to light when Campbell entered 3 Mercedes cars for the Ulster TT Race on the Ards Circuit at Belfast, Ireland, later that year. Driven by the same team, the cars were thought to be of standard production. During the trial runs, Caracciola's speed were far superior to those of his team mates, and when the cars were scrutineered, it was found that the supercharger fitted to Caracciola's car was of greater dimensions than standard. He was given the choice of changing the supercharger or disqualification. He decided on the latter and did not compete.

The picture shows Campbell about to pass Campari's Alfa, No 21, and Oats' OM, No 19.

128 The Napier-Arrol-Aster *Bluebird* was removed to the Brooklands workshops of Thomson & Taylors, adjacent to the Byfleet Banking, during the early winter of 1930, where a new gearbox, clutch and other modifications were to be made, to the designs of Reid Railton, the talented designer who had been working for the late Parry Thomas.

My old friend Joseph Maina had now ceased to work in Campbell's interest and although the FBM gearbox he had designed, after curing its teething troubles, had given little bother and stood up exceedingly well to the increased horsepowers that were applied to lift up our former record attempts, its gear-changing characteristic was never a success. On more than one occasion, Campbell, being unable to engage second gear, would be forced to complete his run using first and top gears only, a distinct disadvantage when, for some reason or other, the length of his run in some cases was reduced by two miles.

The expedition to the Sahara and subsequent exploits at Verneuk Pan had been costly adventures, far in excess of the small contributions that had been made. Even Campbell, although a wealthy man, now fully aware of the mounting costs that the unforeseen delays in these record attempts can bring, had to give this matter some serious thought.

Miss Betty Carstairs, the wealthy everbereted sportswoman who had competed against the American Gar Wood with her speedboats *Estelle I* and *II* was often seen at Brooklands with Campbell. She very sportingly contributed £10,000 towards Campbell's venture.

129 Napier's support for Campbell's new project was not found lacking. Two of their latest Napier Lion engines were placed at our disposal. Now supercharged, but of the same bore x stroke as its predecessor [900hp], this engine developed 1450hp. Its outward appearance remained unchanged, apart from the centrifugal supercharger fitted to the front of the engine.

Railton had ingeniously designed a compact gearbox, which was mounted to the left-hand side of the chassis, allowing sufficient space to accommodate the pilot's seat alongside it, while using the same rear axle, which was modified to suit the now offset drive-shaft. The original dual Marles steering was retained, the steering column being lowered to the horizontal position to conform with the pilot's new seating position. Except for a completely new clutch to cope with the increased power and loading, the front axle, brakes and chassis configuration remained unaltered. On account of the low construction of the completed vehicle, Railton had incorporated four fixed jacking points to facilitate removal of the road wheels - a manoeuvre which had presented problems during our past records.

About mid-November, one cold morning, Charles Brackenbury, driving his old Chrysler, towed me from T&T's, Brooklands, to Gurney Nutting at Lacland Place, Chelsea, where a new body, designed by Pierson of Vickers, was to be constructed and fitted.

The picture shows the completed chassis in T&T's workshop. Starting fourth from left: Reid Railton, Campbell, Thomson and Ken Taylor.

130 The status of Campbell's LSR endeavours in those far-off days can be best assessed by the immense interest shown by the public. But of more importance was the keenness and effort expended by the many who were working on the project. It would be difficult to draw a comparison between the boys of today working on some high speed project and the lads who have worked alongside myself in the past. From my own experiences, I do know that monetary consideration was not the attraction.

With barely a month in which to complete the body, the lads at the coachbuilders, under the supervision of a chap called Piercy [himself a master panel-beater] worked endlessly in shifts, 24 hours a day, and the car was completed during the first week of January 1931. It was towed from the coachbuilders to Messrs Rootes' showrooms in Piccadilly, where it was put on show for a few

days pending its removal to LEP Transport at Chiswick, where a packing case had been made ready for its transportation to the USA.

Here is the completed car at the coachbuilders, prior to its removal.

---

131 The rear view of the Napier-Campbell *Bluebird*. Notice in particular the offset tailfin and the lifting jacks in position.

Some days before we embarked for the United States, the American Automobile Association wired Campbell to delay his departure: the councillors of the City of Daytona would only contribute £800 to the expenses of the timekeepers, who were insisting on 4000 dollars. Strangely, Campbell was not unduly disturbed by the news, possibly having received an appealing invitation from the authorities in New Zealand to run *Bluebird* on a flat stretch of sand known as

90-Mile Beach. On the other hand, the possibility of meeting an unknown challenger known as Norman 'Wizard' Smith gave him good reason to consider the matter in detail on hearing that Smith's car was powered by a Napier engine identical to *Bluebird*'s.

Disregarding all opposition, Campbell, the team, the car with a spare engine, cases of tyres and equipment sailed from Southampton aboard the *SS Homeric* on 14th January 1931.

I had the good fortune to have my old friend Harry Leech with me on this occasion. He had been one of the engineers on board the R101 when it crashed and burst into flames at Beauvais, France, on its maiden voyage. He was one of the four survivors and was awarded the George Model for rescuing one of his comrades from the burning wreck. Joe Coe and Steve MacDonald, with an assistant, were the other members of the team.

132 On arrival at New York and having cleared Customs with our personal belongings the team was driven to the Statler Hotel. The following morning, a representative of American Express called for us and drove us to the docks to clear the car and the numerous cases of tyres, tools and spares that were now scattered over the dockside. It was miserably cold and the lousy Customs officials made us unpack the cases; using the multiple lists we had prepared, they literally checked every item we had brought with us. We thankfully left Pennsylvania Station on the *Dixie Flyer* that evening, arriving at Daytona the following midnight.

When the car arrived by freight train two days later, it was removed from its case and I was towed to the garage that had been reserved as our working quarters. By the time Campbell arrived that evening, we had run the engine and were more or less standing by. The following day, 30th January, we were held up by bad weather. The day after that, Campbell hit 192 mph in a four-mile run. We fortunately had no mechanical setbacks, but were delayed through unfavourable climatic conditions and rough beach surfaces.

The picture shows Campbell discussing the situation with your humble servant. Note the rpm counter cover fitted to the forward engine cover. This enabled the Skipper to check his rpm and maintain his vision ahead without losing the split second of concentration .

---

133 During one of the trial runs, Campbell had a near miss when the car slipped out of gear. He stopped at the end of the course and I drove down with Joe Coe to tow him in. With some concern, he told us that he was probably doing 260 when the gear lever shot back and the needle on the rev counter registered an abnormal rpm. Back at base, the engine was given a thorough check and run-up. By the grace of God, no damage had been done.

Campbell had his sights on increasing the 5-Mile and 5-Kilo records he had set up at Verneuk. But the officials objected to this as they were not in favour of his running between the pylons supporting the pier to obtain a longer run.

Thursday, 5th February, looked hopeful. Once the tide had receded the course was checked, and subsequently markers and the timing strips were laid at both Start and Finish [see picture]. No time was lost and the car was towed to the beach and the tyres, spare fuel, etc, had been despatched to the south end.

The Skipper soon joined us and after the usual Press routine took his place in the cockpit. Having received the all-clear from the officials, with his usual calmness, he lowered his goggles and exclaimed, 'OK, chaps - start her up!' In a dense cloud of black smoke, the engine burst into life and with one-and-all pushing to avoid wheel spin, *Bluebird* sped on her way. Without stopping for a tyre check at the turn-round, he made a wide turn and made his return run.

Campbell had regained his coveted LSR with an average 246.09 mph.

---

134 It was generally taken for granted that Campbell's LSR attempts were to gratify his own personal ambition of being the Fastest Man on Four Wheels. But there was more to it than that. Campbell was a true patriot who loved his King and Country. His slogan, 'All British and Best', was more than just an empty or meaningless phrase. At the time, the English motor industry was going through a bad period. The medium-size cars we were producing to offset the hp tax which existed at

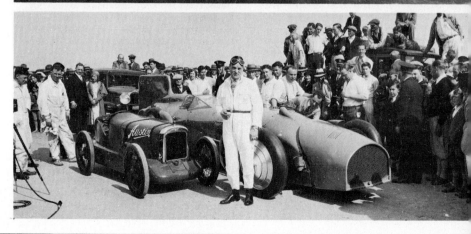

the time were not popular on the foreign markets. To enhance trade and create interest a standard Austin 7hp was tuned up to create a record for its 750cc class. Perhaps it did not quite create the excitement that was accorded to its big brother *Bluebird*, but its average speed for the two runs over the Flying Mile - 94.031 mph - certainly created a very good impression; the previous International Record for that class was 87.76 mph.

Then we received the tragic news that Mr Montagu Napier had died. He was the chairman of D Napier & Son, and had played a major part in the design of the world famous Napier Broad Arrow engine. Montagu Napier had shown a keen interest in Campbell's record achievements, and was influential in making the various Napier engines used in *Bluebird* available. Much to Campbell's regret, he had passed away just four days before this latest LSR, which became an epitaph rather than a tribute.

135 Campbell returned to New York, leaving the team to tuck *Bluebird* into its large packing case, re-crate the equipment and supervise the issue being loaded onto the freight train. We stayed at Daytona for the next two days, relaxing on the beach and being generally entertained before entraining for New York. Campbell was now the idol of the American public and fêted at several stops during his rail journey to New York.

We eventually sailed from New York aboard the old *SS Mauretania*, the old ship that at one time held the Blue Riband for the Atlantic crossing. It was a most enjoyable return and the team were invited to Campbell's first class quarters to take a drink with Charles Chaplin and Steve Donoghue, who were on board at the time. The time schedule went a bit haywire when the ship went aground on entering the Solent. Campbell finished his voyage in the pilot boat in order to be on time to meet the Mayoress and Press at Southampton. We were driven to the station on the following morning and boarded a special private train laid on for Campbell's benefit. This was certainly a hero's welcome home. The crowning glory came when His Majesty King George V bestowed the Order of Knighthood on our Skipper.

136 Campbell, now Sir Malcolm, although advised by his family and many friends to rest on his laurels and live a more leisurely life, was still the same determined cuss he was when I joined him in 1922. He was aware that the potential of his car, the Napier-Campbell, had not been reached. He recalled in particular the valuable seconds that had been lost when the gear shift slipped out of gear on the record run. Nor had he overlooked the other possibility of raising his own 5-Mile and 5-Kilo records. With his mind made up to reach a speed of 300 mph plus, modifications were made to the gearbox, and a more streamlined nose cowl for the radiator was designed and fitted [as shown].

We sailed from Southampton mid-January, leaving the cold and dreary days of an English winter for the sunshine, the orange groves and palmetto trees of Daytona.

The Daytona authorities had removed two of the pier's centre pylons, which gave the Skipper the additional mile and a half so essential for the 5-Mile and 5-Kilo records.

During 24th and 26th February he established a new LSR at 253.968 mph; covered 5 Miles at 242.751 mph; 5 Kilos at 247.941 mph and 10 Kilos at 238.669 mph. For once, we had no mechanical problems.

137 This photograph, taken on the day he set that LSR, shows the wooden structure that was erected to reinforce the section of the pier after the pylons had been removed. The average speed for his 5-Mile and 5-Kilo records would have been reduced had the Skipper been limited to the original course of 9 miles. It was estimated that his speed under the pier on his first run was over 160 mph. Note the firmness of the sand.

Reverting to our activities at Brooklands, Campbell had now purchased the two 4 litre s/c Sunbeams from Wolverhampton - the *Tiger* and *Tigress*. Apart from being more or less on the same design as the car Segrave used at Southport when he set up an LSR, these were the same cars that Kaye Don successfully drove at Brooklands.

They were very fast, weighed less than 1 ton and developed 300hp. Campbell endeavoured to create a record for the Standing Mile with one of them, but was not successful. We ran into many problems and the Skipper was not altogether happy about the fact that they were 10 years old. Reid Railton was consulted and one of the cars was taken to Thomson & Taylor, where, to Railton's design, it was rebuilt.

138 Campbell's interest in competing at Brooklands had now somewhat diminished. He appeared to favour the Mountain Handicap races in place of the Outer Circuit competition. But his main ambition was, of course, to eclipse the magical 300 mph. The Napier-Campbell had been left at Thomson & Taylor and Reid Railton was again to be the brains behind whatsoever the outcome would be.

We had taken delivery of the transformed V12 s/c Sunbeam which now, apart from its engine and rear axle, bore no resemblance to the old *Tiger* or *Tigress*. There was a newly designed chassis, front axle, Lockheed hydraulic brakes, and new suspension all round. While it was being rebuilt at Thomson & Taylor, Armstrong Siddeley had built Campbell a special pre-selector gearbox, which I had fitted. This was a racing-type gearbox and, in particular, it was to prove ideal for the Mountain Circuit. We did experience some trouble with the box and a fellow called Mardlin was sent down to investigate.

I was doing one or two odd jobs to the Sunbeam when Mardlin came over and said, 'Sorry, Leo, I'll have to take the gearbox out'. We worked all night and were still fighting the clock when Campbell arrived, impatient to give the car another run. The picture does not adequately illustrate the stream of eloquence that is flowing between Campbell and myself.

139 Having sorted out its teething troubles, the 4 litre Sunbeam was entered for the 15-Lap Mountain Championship Race. Campbell had pointed out that he considered the mass start across the Finishing Straight did present hazards, and I think the Starting Line was moved back towards the Fork.

The race proved to be an exciting and popular event. Campbell appeared to be in no hurry during the early stages of the race and I was rather concerned that all was not well with the car. But once he got the feel, he certainly gave it the gun and, after a tussle with Raymond Mays, who was driving an Invicta, and Shuttleworth's Bugatti, he took the lead and held it. His average was 68.68 mph with only one lap at 71.39 mph. He failed to beat Birkin's Lap Record speed of 73.51 mph. He told me later that the Wilson pre-selector gearbox, apart from saving valuable seconds, simplified gear changing immensely.

Here is Campbell at the Fork after having overtaken Raymond Mays and Shuttleworth.

SIR MALCOLM CAMPBELL'S SUNBEAM 'TIGER' RACING CAR
En Route LONDON TO BERLIN FOR THE AVUS RACE Via Harwich, Zeebrugge, Brussels, Cologne CONVEYED NON-STOP BY

COMMERCIAL ROADWAYS LTD.

140   I was to make several visits to Thomson & Taylor, where the design and work on Campbell's 300 mph *Bluebird* was going ahead. It was all kept very hush-hush and Ken Taylor, who disliked publicity intensely, appeared to enjoy a great deal of satisfaction having the opportunity of dealing - in anything but a polite manner - with persons caught probing into his workshop.

We did not enjoy a great deal of luck with the Sunbeam he retained, although he had entered it for several events. With Chris Staniland as co-driver, he ran it in the 1000-Mile Race at Brooklands and stood every chance of winning when the drive of the two superchargers packed up. He did, later have the satisfaction of beating Cobb driving his big Delage on Madeira Drive, Brighton.

On another occasion, the Sunbeam was taken to the Avus Track to compete in the Berlin Grand Prix. His chief opponents were Caracciola and Von Brauschitsch. On arrival he was greeted by the ex-Crown Prince of Germany. Campbell's luck ran out on the fourth lap when the engine-scavenging pump failed. Saturated in Castrol 'R', the Skipper ran into the pits, leaving behind a dense cloud of smoke.

141   Possibly the atmosphere of hush-hush and secrecy that was predominant during the construction of Campbell's 300 mph *Bluebird* at Thomson & Taylors was due to the engine that was to be used which, at that period, was more or less on the Air Ministry Secrets List - none other than the R-type Rolls-Royce engine, similar to that used by Flight Lieutenant Stainforth in the Supermarine S6B when he achieved the World's Air Speed Record of 407 mph in 1931. Had it not been for the financial help generously given by Lady Houston to overcome the many problems in completing the R-type, the achievements of our air supremacy in 1931 could never have been accomplished. The R-type was a specially constructed sprint engine, developing 2500hp, supercharged, and with a bore x stroke of 6ins x 6.6ins it was rated at 36,680cc. Rolls-Royce were keen and gave Campbell all the assistance he required.

Railton and Taylor set about the task in a most masterful and economic way; apart from a new sub-frame to carry the engine, the water-cooling capacity was increased and modified and a higher final drive was fitted. The former Amherst Villiers/Joseph Maina design remained unaltered. The picture shows Campbell outside T&T's, trying his seat and controls for size,   Your humble servant is standing by, nursing Campbell's hat and coat.

142   The picture records a memorable moment in T&T's workshop at Brooklands, after the chassis had been completed, and the moment before the Rolls R engine was started for the first time. In attendance were, from left: Reid Railton, Sir Malcolm and Lord Howe, and three of the lads who helped in the car's construction; regrettably, I do not remember their names. On the extreme right of the picture in white overalls is Alf Poyser, the engineer from Rolls, Derby. For the occasion we had to make use of one of our faithful gas starters.

All set, the gas starter was set in motion and the Rolls engine slowly revolved, emitting puffs of petrol vapour. As the exhaust valves on its cylinders opened in a matter of seconds, the engine burst into life, discharging clouds of smoke through its open exhaust ports. This soon cleared and, as the engine settled down to an even rhythm, the blue tongues of flame that were now discharged through the open points indicated perfect carburation.

143 The procedure after the modified chassis construction at T&T's followed more or less the same pattern as the two previous years. The car was transported to Gurney Nutting Ltd to have the new streamlined body [designed by Railton and Pierson of Vickers at Brooklands] constructed and fitted. When this was completed, the car was taken to Campbell's home, Povey Cross, for another check and engine run and a Press Day, when this photograph was taken.

Alf Poyser came down from Rolls at Derby to conduct the engine run and attend to one or two details requiring his attention. The coachbuilders had turned out a remarkably good job, the design being such that, apart from the tail, the complete front section of the body could be removed, giving us complete accessibility to the engine, gearbox, etc.

Subsequently, the car was transported to LEP Transport to be packed into an enormous case that had been custom-built for it.

144 With the huge case containing *Bluebird* securely lashed down on the top deck and our numerous cases of equipment stowed below, we sailed from Southampton during January 1933 on board the *SS Aquitania*. This now seemingly annual excursion to the sunny coast of Florida might have given many a false impression of Campbell's real intentions and purpose. As far as I was concerned, having to leave my wife Joan alone to cope with the rigours of the English winter was the only 'fly in the ointment'.

On arrival in New York we were delayed an extra day before leaving for Daytona. A fair amount of contraband had been smuggled through the Customs and, once again, no exceptions were made; our cases of equipment and spares were minutely examined. We were hanging around those ruddy cold docks for nearly two days. This year, the Hudson & Essex car dealers put their workshop at our disposal and arrangements were made for free public entrance to view the car 24 hours a day. A police guard was maintained throughout.

The picture shows *Bluebird* in the Hudson workshop and the section partitioned off with wire netting. The structure was not particularly robust and to prevent its collapse from the pressure of the viewers leaning on it, we wired one of our starter magnetos to the netting. This did have some remarkable results.

145 Here is *Bluebird*, running down the slipway onto the beach for its first trial run.

Unlike our good fortune and easy record with the Napier the previous year, the 1933 project, apart from the setbacks owing to adverse weather conditions, brought mechanical problems as well. With all the power we had available and the favourable stability the model had shown during its wind tunnel tests, Campbell's target of 300 mph had, unwisely, been a foregone conclusion.

Alf Poyser had now been joined by his colleague George Lovesey, a technical expert from Rolls-Royce, who was in the States at the time. On our first trial run, Campbell, characteristically, asked Poyser the permissible rpm he could run up to. '2000' was Alf's reply. The engine was started and with all of us pushing like hell to prevent wheelspin, he was away.

He ran into trouble before he reached the turn-round, steered the car back and limped back. As the car came to a standstill, acrid smells of hot metal and oil rose from the cockpit. Hurriedly climbing out, Campbell exclaimed,

'Something has bloody well seized up! I was going perfectly, when the car rapidly slowed up. So I turned round and coasted back'.

It was while I was being slowly towed back to the workshop that I noticed the max hand on the rpm counter showed 2300 rpm.

146 On inspection, we noticed that the rear portion of the ball joint, housing the main drive universal joint, to which the torque tube enclosing the cordan shaft was located, was badly discoloured. The rear axle was removed to dismantle the damaged section, revealing that the main ball-race supporting the end of the carden shaft had seized and badly scored the housing that was retaining it. Fortunately, we had a replacement for the ball race, but the damage to its housing did present problems. The matter was taken over by an ardent fan of Campbell's who owned a well-equipped machine shop, and under the guidance of Harry Leech, the interior of the housing was built up and machined.

Three days later, *Bluebird* made another trial run but when Campbell was changing from third to top, the gear lever snicked back and damaged his wrist. He received medical attention for this and a bandage was applied. After one of his trial runs, the Skipper remarked, 'The power I have in hand is incredible, but I lose adhesion at about 3000 rpm and I'm having one hell of a job to hold the bitch on her course!'

On 22nd February, after the worst ride he had ever experienced, Campbell beat his own record by 18.140 mph. It now stood at 272.108. On account of wheelspin, the tyres suffered damage and for the first time he was forced to stop at the turn-round to change all four wheels and tyres.

'Jubilation after the Attempt'. The gent with specs on the left is the then Hon Robin Grosvenor, subsequently the late Duke of Westminster. Others: George Lovesey, Alf Poyser, self, Campbell, Harry Leech, Wal Hicks and Dunlop Mac.

147 We all duly returned home and Campbell did receive a hero's welcome. But, inwardly, he was a very disappointed man. His mind was set on that elusive 300 mph, which he was determined to conquer. He was convinced that the Rolls engine had all the power that was needed. The problem of transmitting it without losing the traction so vital to the car's stability was the poser. The car was returned to T&T's and, after many discussions with the powers-that-be, in particular Reid Railton and Ken Taylor, the car was completely stripped out to ascertain the extent of the modifications that were to be made. It was found that, due to the overload exerted through the transmission on Campbell's final runs, the teeth on the crown wheel and pinion were discoloured and blued, due to the oil film breaking down under severe pressure.

I was to spend much of my time during the latter half of 1933 with Sir Malcolm on board a 90ft motor yacht he purchased called *Freebelle III*, subsequently renamed *Bluebird*. It was well appointed with spacious engine room, in which two 90hp Gleniffer diesel engines were housed.

Although many trips were made to the Continent, in some cases hilarious when many of Campbell's Brooklands friends joined us, I found the life on the ocean wave dull and uninteresting after the excitement and activities of racing and record-breaking.

Here we are on another voyage, snapped by Sir Malcolm. Left to right: Captain Leper, Bill Sturm [originally Segrave's manager and, in later years, organiser of Campbell's attempts] and Leo.

148 I was more than pleased when the Skipper terminated his High Sea exploits later in 1933 and I returned to Brooklands to do some work on the 4 litre s/c Sunbeam which he had entered for the 10-Lap Mountain Championship, scheduled to take place during the BARC closing meeting.

During practice, the car, fortunately for me, came up to 'Sir's' expectations, although he still considered the mass start before reaching the Banking Turn a hazard and dicey. On the day of the event, eight cars, with their engines running and creating one hell of a racket, were impatiently waiting the fall of Ebby's flag. I, as usual, was holding grimly on to one of 'Sir's' twin rear wheels in a futile attempt to prevent him from creeping forward as he was wont to do.

Ebby's flag fell and there was the usual scramble for the Banking Turn; Rose-Richard's Bugatti made it, with Campbell close on his tail. Then it happened. The Bugatti spun off and Campbell shot up the Banking to avoid a collision. But in that split second, the tail end of the Bugatti struck the Sunbeam amidships, causing it to swing completely round and come to a grinding halt in the centre of the track.

I vividly recollect Campbell standing up in the cockpit, excitedly shouting, 'Stop the bloody race!' as the pursuing cars hurtled past. Blue flags were waved to reduce the pace, but some of the drivers pressed on regardless, in particular, Whitney Straight, who won the race. Both cars were seriously damaged. This was to be Campbell's last race with his modified 4 litre Sunbeam, which had originally been the famous *Tiger*.

149 It took the major part of 1933 and 1934 to overcome the many technical problems that arose to re-design and construct a machine that would eventually satisfy Campbell's greatest ambition. At one time, the concept of a four-wheel drive had been given a great deal of thought, but time and costs had to be considered. Apart from this, I feel sure Railton preferred - and wisely - to adhere to the principles on which the former *Bluebirds* had been constructed. Railton, unlike Maina, disliked unnecessary complications. No doubt basing his ideas on past experiences, he realised that, where possible, a simple solution to a problem was more easily found when something went amiss - which it often did.

To conform, a completely new main chassis was built. The old rear and front axles were replaced. A single Burman steering box with orthodox drop arm and track rod replaced the original dual Marles steering layout. Large Hartford shock absorbers were fitted all round and the fuel tank was carried in a cradle on the nearside of the chassis. To increase adhesion of the rear wheels, a substantial number of lead blocks were fitted in the rear end of the chassis for an additional all-up weight. The original braking system was retained, but a large Dewandre vacuum cylinder operating two air-resisting flaps at the tail end of the car reduced the car's forward momentum in the higher speed ranges.

150 After innumerable calculations and expounded theories, Railton had come to the conclusion that by using twin driving wheels and a greatly improved streamlined body, 300+ would be possible. To effect a perfectly streamlined frontal area, a narrow radiator was fitted, extending the full width, under the forward panel's leading edge. The aperture through which the air was conducted to the radiator would be completely closed off by an actuating lever in the cockpit. To prevent overheating, this aperture was to be closed on entering the Measured Mile and opened instantly upon leaving it.

The chassis was completed a bare five weeks before Christmas, then we ran into problems. Campbell was unable to find a coachbuilder who would undertake building the body. Piercy, who had previously worked for Gurney Nutting, would consider tackling the job, with certain provisos, one being its construction in our workshop at Brooklands. Campbell, with no other alternative in mind, accepted Piercy's offer. I had no idea at the time of the difficulties that lay ahead of me. A section of my workshop was set aside for the panel beaters and the now considerably altered chassis of *Bluebird* was towed over from T&T's. Campbell came down to see me the following day and I was given my marching orders. Handing me a chequebook containing several post-dated cheques for specified amounts, he unconcernedly told me he was flying to South West Africa in search of a gold reef and would be away for a brief period.

'Keep the lads at it, old boy. I've booked a passage for us on the *Berengaria* for early January'.

151 Piercy had engaged five panel beaters to assist him, the notable one being George Gray who, at a later date, constructed the body for the late John Cobb's record breaker.

Initially, good progress was made and there was keenness to such an extent that the lads were willing to sleep on makeshift beds in the back of our 2 ton truck should it be necessary. Piercy was not the easiest of persons to get along with, and through one reason or another, progress eased up considerably. I told Piercy I was unhappy about the situation, but he assured me things were well in hand - there was no need to worry. When Campbell returned from the States, I had to explain what was happening - not truly ethical. I had previously aired my grievances with George Gray, who more or less stated had he been in Piercy's shoes, he could cope with the task easily. Campbell came down to Brooklands the following day, saw the poor progress that

had been made, and paid Piercy off. Later, we had an interview with George, who agreed to take over. The ensuing weeks were sheer murder. The boys worked round the clock in shifts. I was to spend many a night sleeping in Campbell's office on the settee. Finally, despite the setbacks and poor conditions then available, the task was completed. On reflection, I do think that 'Sir's' phrase, 'Nothing is impossible' had a ring of truth about it.

The picture shows *Bluebird* after being pushed from our workshop for the first time.

---

152 We sailed from Southampton during January aboard the *Berengaria* for New York. Apart from Dunlop Mac replacing his brother Steve, the team was the same as in 1933. We went through the usual routine as practised over the preceding years and eventually were enjoying the welcome that awaited us on our

arrival at Daytona. It was gratifying to learn that there had been 100% perfect beach conditions during the past weeks. Having unloaded and removed the car from its case at the railhead. It was towed to the Hudson & Essex workshop, where again facilities had been made for the public to view the car.

Campbell made his first trial run after two days' preparation, but we were soon in trouble due to the heat from the short exhaust stubs distorting the side panels that enclosed them and curling their leading edges up like the leaves of a book. The exhaust pipes were lengthened, the panels repaired, and the Skipper was able to make several trial runs during the following day. Owing to the generous free issue of 'Hav-a-Tampa' cigars, the team were being converted into ardent cigar puffers.

The picture shows the activities on the beach prior to 'Sir's' first run.

153 Throughout our stay at Daytona the beach conditions were ideal. We did have other troubles: the Skipper had some difficulty, at speed, locating the marker and starting posts, on account of the glare of the sun on the white sand affecting his vision.

Campbell suggested that a black guideline be laid down the centre of the course, similar to the one we had used at Verneuk Pan. The City Council of Daytona, who were approached, thought Campbell's idea was crazy and impossible, owing to the short period of time, approximately half-an-hour, before the tide turned. But Campbell insisted that it could be done, and pointed out that it was absolutely essential if a new record was to be achieved. No doubt he did give the authorities a headache, but they did eventually knock up a crude arrangement, using old engine oil for the marking line. This, as shown, was a success.

We had our headaches, too - at least, Poyser and Lovesey, the Rolls specialists did. Campbell could not get his maximum rpm in top gear. This was serious.

154 Record-breaking, in many ways, is a frustrating undertaking. Many details have to fit into place before success can be achieved. But seldom, for example, have opportunities been missed when conditions have been perfect. Either the car is receiving some mechanical adjustment or, on the other hand, conditions have held us up for days. There have also been occasions when the timing apparatus malfunctions. At Daytona, the tidal conditions only allow you a limited time to operate. More than once, we have had to tow the car off the beach through shallow water on account of the incoming tide. During our early records we were allowed half-an-hour at the turn-round for a tyre change, refuel, etc. But mechanical changes demanded more operating time and Campbell was successful in getting a new rule passed allowing us 1 hour. Ultimately, when Campbell was compelled to stop after his first run to change his wheels, tyres, etc, an aeroplane was put at our disposal to transport the starting team at the north end to assist the lads at the turn-round.

Fortunately, the beach conditions remained favourable and the Skipper was able to make further trial runs. But although the Rolls specialists spent much of their time checking every detail on the engine, the needle on the rpm counter failed to reach the digit on that instrument which spelled success or failure.

155 We were to learn that one very critical item of the Rolls engine was its main air intake, which was mounted onto the carburation system, facing forward into the main airstream. Much design time and experimentation was expended by Rolls-Royce to produce this intake which, with speeds approaching 300 mph, would produce a ram effect and raise the boost pressure by approximately 4 psi. Harry Leach and myself did think the intake might be a reason for the loss of power, but Poyser and Lovesey did not agree. However, a cable was despatched to Rolls-Royce and their advice was not to alter the intake at any price.

Campbell's term of activities at Daytona was now getting short, so he decided to call in the timekeepers and make a timed run. On 7th March 1935, with perfect conditions, the Skipper made what was to be his last run on the Florida beach that he and his team had come to know so well, and set up a new record of 276.88 mph. The photo shows *Bluebird* on the north-south run, all-out over the Starting Line. It was another record maybe - but not the record he wanted.

156 The following evening, the Skipper gave his team a night out, and we spent much of the evening chatting about our past events. Naturally, he aired his disappointment to us and, like ourselves, was at a loss to understand why that bloody rpm counter needle persisted in wavering around 3000 rpm and not the 3400 we all had so eagerly anticipated. He was still convinced the car could do it, but now realised that the beach at Daytona was getting too short on account of the added all-up weight of the car and the increase in speed that had been anticipated.

'You know, lads, it's fascinating but frightening when you see the rubber casing fly off the outer perimeter of your front tyres, taking the layer of canvas with it! For all the world, it looks like a tyre with three treads. Another thing is the running surface of the tyre, which is almost flat when the car is stationary, but develops an apex due to centrifugal action when at high speed!' He expressed his gratitude for Railton's brilliant design, stating that *Bluebird*, unlike its namesake of 1933, was now infinitely stable.

With more than regrets, we bade farewell to the many kind friends we had the privilege to meet at Daytona and returned home on the largest liner at that time - the *SS Majestic*.

157 Although the Skipper's new record was but marginal, he nevertheless received a Speed King's welcome when we arrived back at Southampton. *Bluebird* was transported to our workshop at Brooklands and 'Sir' made a demonstration run round the Outer Circuit.

During a conversation I had with Reid Railton, I more or less told him of our troubles at Daytona.

'Have you any hunches, Villa?' was his remark. And I told him that some doubts had been entertained about the main air intake. Railton strolled over to the front of the car and, after spending some time studying the radiator aperture, he requested me to operate the lever that closed the flap. After further ponderance, he came over to me and said, 'You know, Villa, you may have a point there'.

The car was later towed over to T&T's and Vickers carried out further wind-tunnel tests.

Press stories circulating, stating that Daytona was now unsuitable for higher speeds, resulted in Campbell receiving a cable from the Chamber of Commerce for Utah, who were prepared to put some facilities at his disposal if he would agree to attempt the record on the Utah Salt Flats. This dried-up section of hard salt, which was at one time a section of a vast expanse of water known as the Great Salt Lakes, is situated about 100 miles from the Mormon headquarters of Salt Lake City. A favourable report from John Cobb, who had been active out there breaking class records with his 23 litre Napier-Railton, induced the Skipper to make his next attempt on the Utah Salt Flats.

158 Wind-tunnel tests by Vickers proved that without a shadow of doubt the airstream realised from the upper aperture, after passing through the radiator slot, was seriously affecting the ram effect, for which purpose the intake was designed. So, hopefully, the intake was lengthened to bridge the aperture. I worked over at T&T's fitting a long box, made by Kodak, containing a duplicate set of instruments and an electrically driven ciné camera. The instrument board was illuminated by a series of bright lights. This was to be set in motion prior to his runs. No doubt, apart from a publicity stunt, the Skipper required this to dispel any doubts that had been aired on some of his observations after his previous records.

159 That ruddy gearbox had me worried and I lost no time removing the inspection cover to find out what had gone amiss. I soon discovered that the first gear had slid along the layshaft and held in mesh. With the aid of a lever, I was able to prise the gear back into its neutral position and all was well. After some consideration and a further check, I came to the conclusion that the gear had been impelled forward due to the violent shunting well known on the American railroad system.

We were taken over to check the Salt Flats by the Chamber of Commerce officials in a large Lincoln car, which was later placed at our disposal. At first sight, the vast expanse of salt was pleasing. But its hard, rough surface did leave room for doubt. On several occasions we gave the Lincoln some rough handling but this had no ill effects to its tyres.

Campbell, with his son Donald, arrived at Wendover some days later, accompanied by Railton and Harry Leach. Wendover, in those days, boasted a motel, which was to be our living quarters, and a restaurant, which straddled the border between Utah and Nevada. After the high class comforts of Daytona, Wendover was anything but attractive. However, our schedule went according to plan and the picture shows the car being towed to the Flats for our first try-out. Note the extended main air intake.

160 A track 12 miles long and 50 yards wide was prepared for *Bluebird*'s attempt. The loose salt ridges covering the surface were scraped away by a heavy steel joist being drawn across the surface and then swept to the side. The only disadvantage was that the Flats were 4218ft above sea level, which would give us a slight loss of hp and, as calculated, reduce the effectiveness of the air flaps. On the other hand, a lessened overall air resistance would be an advantage. By midday, the temperature would soar to 100°, so whenever possible early morning runs were organised.

'Sir' made several trial runs and, apart from one or two minor adjustments, the situation looked a very hopeful one. The black line marked down the centre of the track stood out plain and clear against its background of white salt, and dark tinted sunglasses became a very essential item for all of us. The Skipper accomplished a speed in excess of 240 mph on his first trial run with comparative ease. But the under and topsides of the body were covered in loose dry salt after the run. A temporary awning had been erected at each end of the course to shelter the car and personnel from the sun. The picture shows the activity at the turn-round after a trial run.

161 On the morning of 3rd September the timing officials were at their stations. The record tyres and wheels had been fitted and the Skipper, in a jovial mood, was standing by. After a chat with young Donald, he positioned himself on the side of the cockpit to let Alf Poyser wipe the salt from his shoes, and then settled himself into the cockpit.

The timekeepers had given us the all-clear and the engine was started with all of us pushing like the devil to avoid wheelspin. The car was soon out of sight, leaving behind a black trail of smoke. An aeroplane followed, to take the photo shown.

Donald and I made a dash for the Lincoln and were soon doing 80 mph alongside the track. That 12 miles of salt seemed endless. Donald, like myself, was all tensed up as we passed the timekeepers' station on our left and still another 5 miles to go. Donald muttered something about, 'So far, so good. Can't you go any faster?' I noticed he was clutching the mascot that his father had given him for good luck - a small silver horseshoe.

We finally passed the last marker of the run-up and then spotted *Bluebird*, which had stopped short of the awning specially erected for wheel changing, etc. The Skipper had not followed his usual practice of turning the car about for its return run and, more frightening, there was a pall of smoke rising from the nearside front wheel.

162   When the Lincoln came to a standstill, Donald went over to his father, who was standing some distance away from the car, looking pale and shaken. The team was attempting to remove the wheel and tyre which, due to a blow-out when leaving the Measured Mile, was well and truly alight. Water was poured over fiercely burning pieces of canvas and rubber that had become lodged in the damaged wheel-fairing. Fortunately, Eyston's co-driver and mechanic, Bert Denley, was there and was most helpful. To remove the still burning wheel, we had to cut away some of the damaged fairing that restricted its removal. We finally succeeded and by the time all four wheels had been changed and the car refuelled, the Skipper had regained some of his composure and told us he had definitely exceeded 300 mph on the run-up, but was in dire difficulties when he closed the radiator shutter on entering the Measured Mile. At that point, exhaust fumes filled the cockpit and seriously affected his breathing and vision. Time was slipping by when we were alerted to hold the Skipper back as they were having trouble with the timing apparatus.

With barely 7 minutes of the specified hour left, we received the all-clear. The engine was started. After turning the car in a wide arc, *Bluebird* again straddled the black line and the Skipper was on his return run.

163   Following in *Bluebird*'s wake in the Lincoln on the return journey with young Donald was a most miserable interlude. Even at 80 mph, 12 miles allows you more than enough time to brood over the many things that could happen to curtail an ambition that your employer has cherished for a number of years. Sheer guts and determination overcame the fears he must have experienced on his first run and gave him the courage to get back into that cockpit and make his return run.

When we arrived back at base, we thankfully saw the Skipper surrounded by the Press, now in a jovial mood and looking his old self

164   Apparently, when the Skipper eased himself from the cockpit after his return run he was cheered and given a great ovation by the Press and many who had gathered round the car. 'You've averaged over 300 mph!' was the general acknowledgment.

When Donald and I reached base, Donald ran over and hugged his father, who at the time was talking to Reid Railton. Campbell then called the team together and, with his usual expression, 'Bloody good show, chaps!' thanked us all sincerely for the part we had played. Then came the anti-climax. Otis Porter, the chief AAA timekeeper with Ted Allen, came over with the disappointing news that his actual average speed for the two runs was 299.874 mph - not 300 plus, as was generally announced. The jubilant atmosphere was now no more and after a consultation with Reid Railton, the Skipper decided to make another attempt the following morning. I was towed back in *Bluebird* to Wendover.

The photo shows *Bluebird* with Campbell all smiles before receiving the bad news.

165 While the Dunlop boys were preparing two sets of wheels and tyres for the contemplated re-run the following morning, the other members of the team were making an extensive check of the vital parts of the machine, in particular the front nearside hub, which, apart from the intense heat generated by the burning tyre, could have been subject to severe overload, resulting from the out-of-balance forces of the deflated tyre. We had probably been working for about two hours when the Skipper and Railton walked into the garage. Loudly, the Skipper exclaimed, 'All right, lads, call it a day! I shall not be running in the morning after all. The timekeepers made a cock-up in their calculations and my average speed was 301.129 mph. In fact, my average on the first run was 304.31!' He then lamented that the error made had dimmed the sense of satisfaction he would have enjoyed to the full had that miscalculation not occurred. And once more, as he was leaving the garage, was to hear his old familiar expression, 'Ah well, such is life'. At the time, he was in his fiftieth year and this was to be his final Land Speed Record.

---

166 In direct comparison with my former boss, Giulio Foresti, initially I found Campbell a very difficult man to get along with. With a fiery Scottish temperament, he gave no quarter and expected none. He was exacting in the extreme and could consider nothing impossible. His great wealth allowed him to indulge in a very strict form of independence. He often commented, 'Don't believe in trash'. In some quarters he was considered mean. His point of view, quoted at me many a time, was, 'Villa, money doesn't grow on trees'.

Possibly his first wife's disloyal adultery with his business partner whilst he was patriotically serving his King and Country on the Western Front, had left Campbell an embittered but firm adherent to that now forgotten quality known as loyalty. This he expected above all from me during our joint endeavours. 'Loyalty you cannot buy,' he often said. Although extremely possessive, his great characteristics were guts and determination.

Superstitious by nature, having named all his vehicles *Bluebird* on the advice of a mystical Belgian playwright, Campbell once confessed to me, 'There is more attached to the stars than we shall ever know about, Leo'. This photograph, taken during an unguarded moment, catches the inner self of the man I grew to admire.

---

167 With Malcolm's passing, I was to work with his son Donald. Unlike his father, Donald was less wealthy, more generous, and not as exacting, and would always find an excuse to cover our misfortunes when things went wrong. He often used the phrase, 'Don't worry, Unc - something is bound to turn up'. On the other hand, he had inherited the guts, determination and superstition of his father.

This photograph was taken by Edward, Lord Montagu of Beaulieu, at Goodwood in 1960. The car on the left you may recognise as the 350hp Sunbeam with which Donald's father established those early Land Speed Records in the 1920s. By comparison, the Proteus jet driven car on the right is the CN7, which was the first car driven by Donald to establish a speed of over 400 mph across Lake Eyre, South Australia, almost 30 years after his father had eclipsed the 300 mph barrier at the Utah Salt Flats. CN7 developed approximately twice the horsepower of the Campbell-Railton, although weighing approximately half a ton less. But by this time your humble servant had moved into the Jet Age - and he's never been the same since.

168 *Postscript.* In Spring 1978, Leo's wife Joan died of cancer after 54 years of happy marriage. In the months that followed, despite loneliness, severe depression, weight loss and lung problems, Leo painstakingly applied himself to writing this *KALEIDOSCOPE.* Always aiming for perfection, he sometimes re-wrote certain captions three times. Soon after its completion in November he was admitted to Redhill General Hospital.

When I visited him on Wednesday, 17th January, I found Leo very emaciated, but with his mind 100% alert, wanting to know when he would be able to check over the printer's proofs of his book. His death on that Thursday morning tragically denied him that challenge.

Over 50 people attended his Cremation, despite severe snow and rail strikes.

But the story does not end there. In June 1979, Leo's nephew, Phil Villa, married Gina, the daughter of Donald Campbell - and the partnership now enters into its third generation.

KEVIN DESMOND

Published by: Published by: Marshall Harris & Baldwin Ltd.
17 Air Street
London, W.1.

Registered in London 1410311.

Designed by Brian Harris and Mark Slade

Printed by: Blackwells of Oxford